T0360633

Accounting, Representation and Responsibility

In organizations, accounting produces organizational knowledge that affects decision-making and managerial action. Companies placing importance on shareholder value sometimes tend to elevate accounting to a higher truth criterion for justifying managerial actions. Yet, the nature of accounting renders it difficult to argue that accounting information necessarily produces a better basis for decision-making than arguments which are not based on accounting. This is because, as previous research has also argued, accounting counts some things but omits many others, while managers are accountable for much more than what accounting actually counts.

Using a theoretical apparatus from Deleuze and Guattari, this book illustrates that accounting-based actions such as making management decisions, maintaining organizational responsibility and hierarchical control are manifestations of the ways in which accounting is composed. This concise introduction will be invaluable for researchers and advanced students of management accounting exploring responsibility accounting and accountability.

Niels Joseph Lennon has a Ph.D. from Copenhagen Business School, Denmark, and is currently Associate Professor at Aalborg University, Denmark. He is interested in performance measurement, especially how accounting calculations construct visualizations of organizations and how such visualizations affect decision-making and managerial action.

Routledge Focus on Accounting and Auditing

Advances in the fields of accounting and auditing as areas of research and education, alongside shifts in the global economy, present a constantly shifting environment. This presents challenges for scholars and practitioners trying to keep up with the latest important insights in both theory and professional practice. Routledge Focus on Accounting and Auditing presents concise texts on key topics in the world of accounting research.

Individually, each title in the series provides coverage of a key topic in accounting and auditing, while collectively, the series forms a comprehensive collection across the discipline of accounting.

The Boundaries in Financial and Non-Financial Reporting
A Comparative Analysis of their Constitutive Role
Laura Girella

The Future of Auditing
David Hay

Accounting Regulation in Japan
Evolution and Development from 2001 to 2015
Masatsugu Sanada and Yoshihiro Tokuga

Gender and Corporate Governance
Francisco Bravo Urquiza and Nuria Reguera-Alvarado

Accounting, Representation and Responsibility
Deleuze and Guattarí Perspectives
Niels Joseph Lennon

For more information about the series, please visit www.routledge.com/
Routledge-Focus-on-Accounting-and-Auditing/book-series/RFAA

Accounting, Representation and Responsibility
Deleuze and Guattarí Perspectives

Niels Joseph Lennon

Routledge
Taylor & Francis Group

LONDON AND NEW YORK

First published 2021
by Routledge
2 Park Square, Milton Park, Abingdon, Oxon OX14 4RN

and by Routledge
52 Vanderbilt Avenue, New York, NY 10017

Routledge is an imprint of the Taylor & Francis Group, an informa business

British Library Cataloguing-in-Publication Data
A catalogue record for this book is available from the British Library

Library of Congress Cataloging-in-Publication Data
Names: Lennon, Niels Joseph, author.
Title: Accounting, representation and responsibility : Deleuze
and Guattari perspectives / Niels Joseph Lennon.
Description: Abingdon, Oxon; New York, NY: Routledge, 2021. |
Series: Routledge focus on accounting and auditing |
Includes bibliographical references and index.
Identifiers: LCCN 2020013889 (print) | LCCN 2020013890 (ebook) |
ISBN 9780367136017 (hardback) | ISBN 9780367136024 (ebook)
Subjects: LCSH: Accounting—Philosophy. | Decision making. |
Responsibility accounting. | Managerial accounting.
Classification: LCC HF5625 .L46 2021 (print) | LCC HF5625
(ebook) | DDC 657.01—dc23
LC record available at https://lccn.loc.gov/2020013889
LC ebook record available at https://lccn.loc.gov/2020013890

ISBN: 978-0-367-13601-7 (hbk)
ISBN: 978-0-367-13602-4 (ebk)

Typeset in Times New Roman
by codeMantra

Contents

Acknowledgments

Writing this book has only been possible due to many discussions with great colleagues. My thanks therefore go to my colleagues at Copenhagen Business School, who have listened to my ideas and shaped my arguments. I also want to acknowledge helpful comments made by participants at the Interdisciplinary Perspectives on Accounting Conference in Stockholm (2015), where parts of the book were presented.

During the writing up of the manuscript, I owe a very big thanks to my colleagues at Aalborg University – especially Thomas Borup Kristensen and Niels Sandalgaard, who gave me space to concentrate on this work while teaching and supervision pressed on. At Aalborg University, I also owe a very big thanks to Kasper Trolle Elmholdt, who shares my theoretical interests in Deleuze and Guattari's writings. Kasper has always been very helpful and open to both discussing and reading my more or less unfinished work. Kasper read all the chapters in their entirety and came up with great suggestions to improve the arguments throughout. Therefore, he deserves major credit for quality of the book, of course, without bearing any responsibility for its shortcomings.

Part I

Theoretical plateaus

1   Introduction

In our everyday lives we are surrounded by different elements and things. These, as obvious as they seem in our everyday lives, can theoretically be understood as signs that our minds decode and assign with meaning. In his work with Felix Guattarí, the French philosopher Gilles Deleuze offers some postmodern theoretical concepts to understand how this process works (Deleuze, 2004; Deleuze & Guattarí, 2004). Accounting is no different than other elements and things we engage with. Accounting information acts essentially as signs that users, whether they are accountants, top-level managers or lower level managers/decision makers, decode with a meaning; the actor signifies the sign. Through the process of signification, the user creates an understanding of the message that the accounting calculation provides. This is the accounting ontology I unfold in this book. In that way, the book offers an alternative, postmodern view on accounting that differs from the mainstream idea of 'accounting as representation' (Ijiri, 1975; Ryan, Scapens, & Theobald, 2002).

The postmodern literature has already shown the importance of understanding how an accounting sign[1] is formed through processes of fabrication in order to understand its organizational and social effects (Chua, 1995; Preston, Cooper, & Coombs, 1992; Robson, 1992). Postmodernism turned causality upside down by arguing that in order to create effects, accounting (as well as other inscriptions) assembles a collective network of relations in organizations, and the organizational effects are therefore mediated by the composition of this collective.

However, while the present postmodern literature proves this point well, the process of signifying accounting information – that is, the process by which users ascribe meaning to accounting information – also affects managerial action and decision-making in non-intentional, non-prescriptive ways. This aspect of postmodern thought is not yet described in the accounting literature. In short, signification of signs happens within a regime that together conditions how the sign is signified.

This book focuses on these processes of engaging with accounting information and signifying the meaning of this information to use it to guide managerial action. I do so by studying the role accounting plays in managerial action in a responsibility center, where accounting information is used for accountability purposes.

Accountability

Accountability is the act of giving and receiving accounts of one's conduct and has deep roots in Western culture (Munro, 1996). One central way of rendering people in organizations accountable is to construct accounts of their conduct, for example, through responsibility accounting. Due to the central role accountability plays in accounting for control (Zimmerman, 2011), the literature has discussed accountability from a variety of theoretical points of views, including financial considerations (Ijiri, 1975), ethics (Messner, 2009; Roberts, 2009), management technologies (Kirk & Mouritsen, 1996) and accountability as an everyday practice, with deep roots in the construction of society (Munro, 1996). Another, related, stream of accounting literature describes responsibility accounting as a method to render business unit managers accountable.

Responsibility accounting treats economic responsibility through delegation. The organization delegates a particular part of a budget to the manager in charge of a business unit. Thereby, this manager is in principle evaluated based on one single number, dependent on which kind of responsibility center the manager is in charge of; these numbers can be revenue, costs, profit, return on investment (ROI), economic value added (EVA) or other measures. The idea of this is to hold the manager responsible for the decisions he or she makes in accordance with the decision rights, the responsibility center is assigned. Thus, accountability is measured in terms of the decisions' effects on financial numbers (Zimmerman, 2011).

On the practical side, responsibility accounting is about constructing business units in which managers are held responsible for (parts of) the business unit's finances. Briefly, if a manager has decision rights over both the revenue and the cost side of the business unit, it is a profit center. If the manager has control over the cost side only, it is a cost center; and if the manager can control revenue exclusively, but does not have decision rights over the cost side of the business unit, it is a revenue center. If the manager has decision rights over investments within the business unit, it is considered to be an investment center. Then, as mentioned, the different responsibility centers are made responsible for certain financial figures according to which responsibility center it is. An investment center is typically responsible for ROI, residual income or EVA; a profit center is responsible for profit (revenue – controllable costs of operations) (Merchant & Van der Stede, 2007) and a revenue center is responsible for the revenue line, its profit and loss statement, but typically cannot control the cost side and thus is not responsible for that part (Merchant & Van der Stede, 2007; Zimmerman, 2011).

Purpose and contribution of this book

The purpose of this book, which focuses on the themes of accounting, representation and responsibility, is to zoom in on what responsibility means in an accounting context. Accounting is by the functionalist, mainstream research perspective often understood as a practice of representation. However, when closely examining the practice of accounting as a technology for rendering people in organizations responsible, it soon becomes visible that this process of representing certain things through accounts works differently than what the theory of representation would suggest. Our aim is to show that accounting does not represent performance, customer behavior or other social phenomena as the representation theory would suggest. Rather, it presents these things in new and surprising (and often contradictory and conflicting) ways. Thus, accounting certainly has the capacity to render people accountable through numbers, but this accountability, and what it means for managers to be accountable, is significantly different from what conventional theory suggests.[2]

Thus, this focus means that our attempt is to describe more deeply how accounting, representativity and accountability relate. I do so by studying how managers' decision space is constructed and deconstructed by various objects in the practice in which the managers operate. Our claim is that the signification of accounting information is affected by these objects that managers engage with in their daily work.

More specifically, the book contributes by examining how accounting mobilizes a certain version of what it means to be accountable, but accountability is a network of relations in many different, and often contradictory, directions. This goes against accounting as representation because these relations mean that accounting does not represent certain things, but it presents in a new version of these things, often through numbers, calculations (e.g., ratios and other performance indicators) and other kinds of visualizations of performance (graphs, trends, colors of different variance levels and so on).

Thus, accounting is composed of heterogeneous circumstances that shape managers' decision opportunities and space of possible actions (decision space), and, as a result, the accounting version of managers' accountability is generalized and sometimes disconnected from the reality in which it is mobilized. In popular terms, one could say that accounting counts some matters and leaves other out, but accountability is a broader social phenomenon related to the accountable subject, and its composition is exterior with relations in many different directions that the subjects must think about.

Notes

1 Accounting signs are often called accounting 'inscriptions' in this stream of research.
2 'Conventional' refers to mainstream, functionalist accounting theory.

References

Chua, W. F. (1995). Experts, networks and inscriptions in the fabrication of accounting images: A story of the representation of three public hospitals. *Accounting, Organizations and Society, 20*(2/3), 111–145.

Deleuze, G. (2004). *Difference and Repetition*. New York, NY: Continuum.

Deleuze, G., & Guattari, F. (2004). *A Thousand Plateaus*. New York, NY: Continuum.

Ijiri, Y. (1975). *Theory of Accounting Measurement*. Sarasota, FL: American Accounting Association.

Kirk, K., & Mouritsen, J. (1996). Spaces of Accountability: Accounting Systems and Systems of Accountability in a Multinational. In R. Munro & J. Mouritsen (Eds.), *Accountability. Power, Ethos and Technologies of Managing* (201–224). London: International Thomson Business Press.

Merchant, K. A., & Van der Stede, W. A. (2007). *Management Control Systems*. Upper Saddle River, NJ: Prentice Hall.

Messner, M. (2009). The limits of accountability. *Accounting, Organizations and Society, 34*(8), 918–938.

Munro, R. (1996). Alignment and Identity Work: The Study of Accounts and Accountability. In R. Munro & J. Mouritsen (Eds.), *Accountability. Power, Ethos and Technologies of Managing* (1–19). London: International Thomson Business Press.

Preston, A. M., Cooper, D. J., & Coombs, R. W. (1992). Fabricating budgets: A study of the production of management budgeting in the national health service. *Accounting, Organizations and Society, 17*(6), 561–593.

Roberts, J. (2009). No one is perfect: The limits of transparency and an ethic for 'intelligent' accountability. *Accounting, Organizations and Society, 34*(8), 957–970.

Robson, K. (1992). Accounting numbers as "inscription": Action at a distance and the development of accounting. *Accounting, Organizations and Society, 17*(7), 685–708.

Ryan, R., Scapens, R. W., & Theobald, M. (2002). *Research Methods and Methodology in Accounting and Finance*. London: Thomson.

Zimmerman, J. L. (2011). *Accounting for Decision Making and Control* (7th ed.). New York, NY: McGraw-Hill.

2 What can accounting learn from Deleuze?

Post-structuralist research has informed accounting since the first research papers were published toward the end of the 1980s and the start of the 1990s, after Hopwood's call for more contextual and organizational-focused accounting research (Hopwood, 1978, 1983). The journal *Accounting, Organizations and Society* played an important role in directing accounting research toward that end (see Miller & Oleary, 1987; Miller & Rose, 1990; Robson, 1991, 1992 as examples of this turn). Since then, research incorporating insights from post-structuralist thought has grown steadily and actor-network theory (ANT) has become a major theoretical inspiration. The seminal paper by Robson (1991), which included the notion of translation in accounting, became a landmark due to its ambition and potential to expand our knowledge about what accounting does in organizational and managerial practice and in society at large, a perspective that provided significant new insights about accounting. This was followed up by a number of publications drawing on the perspective of ANT (such as Chua, 1995; Mouritsen & Bekke, 1997; Preston, Cooper, & Coombs, 1992; Robson, 1992).

ANT may be considered as extending the lines of post-structuralist thinkers such as Foucault, Serres and Deleuze, affording an empirical or ethnographic version of post-structuralist thought (Law, 2009; Mol, 2005). Deleuze was a major influence in the post-structuralist literature and also a great inspiration to ANT. Yet, in accounting, researchers have been reluctant to do research inspired by Deleuze's scholarship, and only few papers draw explicitly on Deleuze's scholarship (Martinez, 2011; Martinez & Cooper, 2017; Neu, Everett, & Rahaman, 2009). It is our contention that many new insights may be provided by exploring continuities and discontinuities between Latour's ANT and Deleuze's theory on assemblage in relation to accounting. As such, this chapter will describe assemblage theory and how it is used to study responsibility accounting in the empirical case later in the book.

Assemblage theory emerged in Gilles Deleuze's work and his collaboration with Felix Guattarí (Deleuze, 2004; Deleuze & Guattarí, 2004) and was extended in Manuel DeLanda's *Assemblage Theory* (DeLanda, 2006). This line of thought will be connected to the organizing properties of accounting as described by Miller and Power (2013).

Assemblage theory

Assemblage theory and Deleuzian scholarship are used here to broaden the understanding of accounting's effects in practice. Through the notion of sign-signification relationship, assemblage theory covers some of the same concerns as the notion of interpretation in the influential interpretivist research agenda. Yet, there are important differences (Deleuze, 2004), which will be discussed later. Due to this similarity, assemblage theory can arguably bridge the interests of the constructivist perspective with the interests of interpretive research (Chua, 1986).

Assemblage theory gives a theoretical apparatus where the network mindset, which is also articulated in Latour's work (e.g., Latour, 1987, 2005), is considered alongside the concerns of the construction of meaning and how this influences action (Chua, 1986). However, the difference between assemblage theory and the social constructivist concept of interpretation is mainly that, as Latour (2005) also notes, significations are not considered social cognitive constructions designed to explain phenomena that are otherwise difficult to explain, such as culture, but rather significations are ontological constructions which emerge as effects of relations.

An important concern in assemblage theory is that the assemblage of relations forms a regime of signs within which individuals act and within which significations of signs emerge. By understanding signification this way, assemblage theory differs from that of social constructivism's influential concept of interpretive flexibility. Interpretive flexibility means that "the empirical observations and the purposes of technology scientists and engineers refer to, allow different interpretations to a certain degree" (Meyer & Schulz-Schaeffer, 2006, p. 26). In social construction of technology (SCOT), which Pinch and Bijker pioneered, the concept of interpretive flexibility relates, according to Meyer and Schulz-Schaeffer (2006), to the usefulness of technology. In this way, interpretive flexibility is interested in showing how meanings associated with technology are the same within social groups but may vary between groups; hence, interpretations of the meaning of a technology are effects of intergroup negotiations and reduction of the interpretive flexibility of the technology (Klein & Kleinman, 2002;

Meyer & Schulz-Schaeffer, 2006). Interpretive flexibility is based on relativism (Klein & Kleinman, 2002), which implies that

> technology design is an open process that can produce different outcomes depending on the social circumstances of development. Some sociologists of science argue that the very entities of physics, such as the particles studied in particle physics, are the products of intergroup negotiations over the interpretation of observations.

Consensus is an important concern in relation to interpretive flexibility. The technology develops openly and relatively based on the social group that engages with its design. Interpretation therefore explains the relativism component: it explains design concerns that the researcher cannot account for. Consequently, keywords for interpretive flexibility are 'consensus' and 'relativism', whereas for ANT and assemblage theory, they are 'controversy' and 'relationalism'. These are important distinctions because in assemblage theory, technology stabilizes not through social negotiations and consensus building but by enrollments and translations that mobilize the technology and, thus, materialize in ways people can live with (see, e.g., Preston, Cooper, & Coombs, 1992; Robson, 1991, 1992). Put differently, an accounting number cannot be said to be shaped, at the outset, by different occupations or different cultural backgrounds (being a manager, being an employee) but as a result of heterogeneous translations and due to its multiple relations. Hence, the network establishes enough power to convince people about its significance through the enrollment of actors that translates its performance (here we often see the controversy).

As such, signification in the Deleuzian version differs slightly from conventional interpretive research as its conceptualization of meaning constructions is consistent with the ontology of networks in, for example, ANT. Rather than using the notion of interpretation and social construction to explain what cannot be theorized through the concerns raised in the empirical data, the theory uses the assemblage approach to conceptualize how meanings are constructed and how meanings become strategic. As such, the work of Deleuze offers concepts to understand how significations of signs are constructed through regimes of signification. The wording 'signification' is an explicit choice here, as it calls for understanding meaning and the construction of meaning differently. Signification is less 'interpretive' but based on the same principles of networks (réseaux) or assemblages. Signification is therefore considered not a social construction but, rather, a construction to be understood by its relations of exteriority.

By mobilizing assemblage theory, which subscribes to relationalism rather than relativism, the point is that meaning does not come about because of the flexible interpretive capacities of accounting numbers, but signification comes about by enrollment in signifying regimes and translation. Thus, signification is an effect of the relations the technology constructs in the assemblages in which it is signified. In this way, the theories of Deleuze (2004), Deleuze and Guattari (2004) and DeLanda (2006) provide concepts that make it possible to obtain new insights about how accounting technologies unfold in organizations, for instance, how they become important as organizing elements (Hopwood, 1978, 1983). This is in line with Miller and Power (2013) who argue that "organizing without accounting is increasingly unthinkable today, accounting also makes organizing thinkable and actionable in a particular way", and we may add, the effects of accounting as organizing being effects of assemblages of signification. In sum, Deleuze's theory is able to offer a conceptual frame of analysis where significations, as a production in the minds of human beings, are also at stake. This signification is not explicitly developed in ANT, but here we see how it can provide new insights about accounting in practice.

What are assemblages?

Assemblage is a central concept in our analysis and requires elaboration. DeLanda (2006) explains how assemblage theory extends the analytical level from being concentrated on the particularity of objects to also concern larger entities such as interpersonal networks or institutional organizations:

> Assemblages, being wholes whose properties emerge from the interactions between parts, can be used to model any of these intermediate entities: interpersonal networks and institutional organizations are assemblages of people; social justice movements are assemblages of several networked communities; central governments are assemblages of several organizations; cities are assemblages of people, networks, organizations, as well as of a variety of infrastructural components, from buildings and streets to conduits for matter and energy flows; nation states are assemblages of cities, the geographical regions organized by cities, and the provinces that several such regions form.
>
> (DeLanda, 2006, p. 5)

Building on DeLanda, we may consider an assemblage as different modes of organized wholes where an industrial, public or private organization is one example and an accounting representation is another, yet, still entwined with the organization (Miller & Power, 2013). To introduce assemblage theory in the study of the practical significance of accounting technologies helps to understand how the effects of accounting technologies emerge within the assemblage and the significations of calculations. In this sense, the frame of analysis is not limited to study objects and their relations to one another, but it also directs an analytical view on the signification of objects – how organizational members construct certain understandings of what calculations (re-)present (see Chua, 1995, for an elaboration on accounting representation and re-presentation). Again, we have to keep in mind that constructing meaning and representations is not a matter of certain occupational memberships of 'invented' explanations, such as different cultures, but a relational momentary accomplishment of an assemblage. While these representations enact an assemblage, a sort of organizational form, they also have important organizing properties (Miller & Power, 2013).

Assemblage theory is correspondingly interesting because of its emphasis on extending the analytical approach in a way that allows us to study how technologies perform in practice. It does so through a set of concepts that allow, to a larger degree, to study multiplicity and movement within the particularity of the practice through which technologies are mobilized. Assemblage theory aims not to understand the part/whole relationship as mechanistic totalities with interior relations, but rather to study how the assemblage creates a nexus of relations in the organization that it unfolds within and thereby how the relations of the assemblage, qua their particularity, change its significance and modus operandi. In this way, assemblage theory is more interested in entities' capacities and the movements of the assemblage, rather than their properties or characteristics. This line of thought is consistent with our understanding of accounting representations as inherently entwined with organizing (Miller & Power, 2013). Moreover, assemblage theory shares ANT's ontology that no inherent essence of objects exists. The significance of objects is constructed in the assemblage and will, therefore, be different between different assemblages (DeLanda, 2006). Building on Deleuze's theoretical apparatus, assemblage theory pays attention to multiplicity and heterogeneity of assemblages and their effects on performance. The theory is very explicit about the role of capacities of objects – which is conceptualized by the concern that everything is treated as a sign and the significance of a sign is a matter of decoding what the sign means, or its mode of operation – where the assemblages in which the significations unfold also constitute the assemblage of the signification. Deleuze and Guattarí treat this under the notion of regimes of signs and sometimes signifying regimes (Deleuze & Guattarí, 2004).

In sum, through its theoretical focus on movements and becomings, assemblage theory gains significance in analysis. Accounting research that draws on assemblage theory can extend the insights from mainstream accounting research, and also constructivist accounting research, by focusing on the particularity of practice and the role significations of objects play in relation to describing how and why technologies produce the effects they do (Martinez, 2011; Martinez & Cooper, 2017; Neu et al., 2009).

In what follows, I will describe the following Deleuzian concepts related to assemblage theory: the rhizome; sign, signification and regimes of signs; assemblage, territorialization, de- and reterritorialization; and lines of flight and lines of active destruction.

The rhizome

The rhizome is a concept through which it is possible to explain the movements of social phenomena. In biological terms, the rhizome refers to a certain part of some plants close to their roots. The rhizome is, under certain conditions, able to reproduce the plant vegetatively. If even a very small part of the rhizome is removed and planted elsewhere, the plant can reproduce itself there. If an animal eats part of the rhizome, it might disperse small parts of the rhizome on the ground and reproduce the plant as new plants. The implication is that it is impossible to anticipate where the plant will reproduce and which connections the plant will make to other entities (Deleuze & Guattarí, 2004, p. 7). The concept of the rhizome is developed by Deleuze and Guattarí (2004), who explain its use of the term as follows:

It is tracings that must be put on the map, not the opposite. In contrast to centered (even polycentric) systems with hierarchical modes of communication and preestablished paths, the rhizome is an acentered, nonhierarchical, nonsignifying system ... the rhizome has no beginning and no end; it is always the middle, between things, interbeing, intermezzo. The tree is filiation, but the rhizome is alliance, uniquely alliance. The tree imposes the verb "to be", but the fabric of the rhi- zome is the conjunction ... This conjunction carries enough force to shake and uproot the verb "to be".

(Deleuze and Guattarí, 2004, pp. 23 and 27)

The rhizome conceptualizes continuous becoming, a becoming that comes from the acentered conjunctions (links or relations) that move the assemblage rhizomatically without underlying structural order. The rhizome is, as Deleuze and Guattarí (2004) state in the quote, to be contrasted with centered systems. It is acentered and nonhierarchical.

The authors argue that the rhizome contradicts the root-tree, which is organized with a root system, a trunk, branches and leaves. This structure organizes the tree. However, Deleuze and Guattarí argue that the root system and the rhizome are always intermingled with each other and cannot be understood as two opposite models. The two are always present at the same time: one as the structural organizing model (the root-tree) and the other as continuous movements in relation to the particularity in which it operates (the rhizome). Plants provide the example; even when they have a root, trunk and branches, they also have an outside that constructs a rhizome with the wind, animals and humans. In terms of accounting and management control, this means that accounting signifies a structural organized system – the accounting system – but this system has an outside that connects with the particular (the specific context). Thus, the performance of the structural system is realized by the structure and its rhizomatic side, which moves the performance according to the rhizomatic conjunctions it is exposed to. Thus, both the signifying structure of the accounting system and the nonsignifying rhizomatic movements coexist, and the performance of the accounting system is an effect of both sides of the control system.

> While claiming to be traditional Deleuze nevertheless defines philosophy in an unusual way as the art of forming, inventing and fabricating concepts (Deleuze and Guattarí, 1994, p. 2). It has nothing to do with contemplation, reflection, or communication (ibid., p. 6). At its deepest level it is the creation of concepts ... This description suggests the famous rhizome concept, a multiplicity whose parts are interconnected but not according to an underlying structural order, where connections can be made at any point to any point, where new branches can grow and old ones regenerate and reconnect. The rhizome is an image of what philosophy should be, a complex, ungovernable place of spontaneous encounters and devisings standing in sharp contrast to all the efforts of systems of established power to capture, block, channel and control the force it expresses.
>
> (Heywood, 2002, p. 373)

This quote explains that the rhizome contrasts with all systems of established power. But equally important, it shows that we need an empirical awareness when mobilizing the concept of the rhizome in accounting research. This highlights that we cannot take anything for granted or use general structures as explanatory variables – here the different to interpretivism also becomes visible.

Heywood (2002) argues that the rhizome is a multiplicity, which resonates Deleuze and Guattarí's (2004, p. 8) "principle of multiplicity". As Deleuze and Guattarí state, within multiplicity, and therefore within the rhizome, there is no axis or taproot. The multiplicity does not have an object or a subject but only "determinations, magnitudes, and dimensions that cannot increase in number without the multiplicity changing in nature" (Deleuze & Guattarí, 2004, p. 9). As a consequence, there are no points in a rhizome that form a structure; its fabric is multiplicity. Thus, the concept exists alongside other signifying structural systems, but the two are entangled in each other in a complex relationship. As an example of the use of the rhizome in social science research, Bidima and Warren (2005) discuss identity through the notion of the rhizome:

> "They [Deleuze and Guattarí] established a perspective ... of thinking, a thinking of the root and of the rhizome. The unique root is one which kills its surroundings whereas the rhizome is a root that extends towards an encounter with other roots". On the basis of this distinction, Glissant challenges atavistic notions of cultures that define their identity in terms of territory, origin, and ancestry. He opposes to this the idea of composite cultures, which, in the image of a rhizome, disregards territories and deemphasizes genealogies and unilinear affiliation, thus giving rein to pluralities.
>
> (Bidima and Warren, 2005, p. 554)

The quote shows how Bidima and Warren (2005), drawing on Glissant, apply the concept of the rhizome to problematize the identity of culture. In the same way, the rhizome is able to explain how management technologies (the general models that can be understood as management technology's taproot) will extend and connect in the particularity they act within, which changes the identity of the particular management technology. This means that we cannot understand two management technologies that build on the same general model, for example, the Balanced Scorecard, as the 'same' in their practical unfolding. Their performances are co-constructed by the rhizomatic connections they develop in the particularity they are mobilized within (the principle of multiplicity). In this way, accounting practice is understood rhizomatically because it connects and moves with the assemblage it constitutes. From the Deleuzoguattarian perspective, the model has two sides that together form its organizational performance. One side of the model is its capacity as a signifying model that prescribes certain actions and performances, and the other side is the rhizomatic one, which challenges and constructs particular becomings of the technology when the signifying model connects with the idiosyncratic particularities of the organization (the particular context in which it is mobilized to work).

Sign, machinic assemblages and regimes of signs

Machinic assemblages and regimes of signs are important concerns to understand the performance of assemblages and the meanings people tend to ascribe to the signs they engage with in their everyday lives. For Deleuze, all things that humans engage with are essentially understood as signs, and when humans produce an understanding of a sign in a certain way, it is done because the mind ascribes a meaning to the sign. Machinic assemblages have an important role in this. Machinic assemblages form the constructs that mediate which meanings are ascribed to signs. This section discusses machinic assemblages and their relation to thought and, thereafter, to regimes of signs.

Machinic assemblages

Deleuze and Guattarí (2004) think about the existence of free statements in their work on machinic assemblages. In their discussion of machinic assemblages, the existence of free will (treated in some places in the scholarship as pure thinking) is questioned. They argue that 'pure thinking' does not exist because statements are always products of machinic assemblages:

> There are no individual statements, only statement-producing machinic assemblages ... For the moment, we will note that assemblages have elements (or multiplicities) of several kinds: human, social, and technical machines ... We can no longer even speak of distinct machines, only of types of interpenetrating multiplicities that at any given moment form a single machinic assemblage ... Each of us is caught up in an assemblage of this kind, and we reproduce its statements when we think we are speaking in our own name; or rather we speak in our own name when we produce its statement.
>
> (Deleuze and Guattarí, 2004, pp. 40–41)

The quote illustrates Deleuze and Guattari's metaphysics about the world, humans and agency. There is, according to Deleuze and Guattari, no free will, no 'pure desire'. There are statement-producing machines (abstract machines) that produce the statements that humans speak. They continue:

> There are no individual statements, there never are. Every statement is the product of a machinic assemblage, in other words, of collective agents of enunciation (take "collective agents" to mean not peoples or societies but multiplicities). The proper name (nom propre) does not designate an individual: it is on the contrary when the individual opens up to the multiplicities pervading him or her, at the outcome of the most severe operation of depersonalization, that he or she acquires his or her true proper name. The proper name is the instantaneous apprehension of a multiplicity.
>
> (Deleuze and Guattari, 2004, p. 42)

Individuals are depersonalized by the multiplicities pervading them, Deleuze and Guattari argue. As such, the thought-experience relationship that happens in humans' minds is a complex assemblage emerging by the multiplicities the human is connected with. Therefore, the notion of machinic assemblages is a counterclaim against the phenomenological ideas of subjectivism and the idea of the human agent as an interpreting actor. As they state, our perception of the world and articulation is constituted by the multiplicities that 'interpenetrate' us and determine our perception of the world.

In accordance with Deleuze and Guattari's work on assemblages, DeLanda (2006) outlines a model of the subject, where the subject emerges as relations of exteriority among contents of experience. In that conceptualization, experience constitutes the representations in memory. But, as discussed previously, this is a synthesis of past assemblages of multiplicities that is not representing the present. It is chains of repetitions that constitute the representational fixity that forms memory, and memory is a generalization of the particularity of the assemblage that the synthesis strived to represent (Deleuze, 1968, p. 91). Thus, memory is also simulacrum, constituted by the passive synthesis of mind. This means that our perception of the world builds on mental representations that themselves are simulacra emerging from synthesis of the past. And these representations frame our perception of the world. In DeLanda's terms, those framings are constructed by social assemblages, which are not to be considered stable, but moving multiplicities that interconnect in the mind of the human. Thus, experience through memory makes us understand things and beings in certain ways as fixities. But the fixities are illusions, the object is always more than the memory's synthesis of it.

Regimes of signs

To understand how accounting representations come to matter and how they become entwined with organizing, we turn to the notion of regimes of signs. As described, machinic assemblages frame our being and understanding of the world. Deleuze and Guattari (2004) devote a chapter (Chapter 5) to the connection between sign and signification, which is at least as important for understanding the theoretical approach to the study as are machinic assemblages. Deleuze and Guattari (2004) write about regimes of signs and the signifiant (signal) and signifié relationship (the generation of the meaning of the sign). The notion of regimes of signs explains the relationship between signifiant and signifié. As mentioned, signs are assemblages of multiplicities, and, thus, the sign is not understood as a sign of a thing:

> Why retain the word sign for these regimes, which formalize an expression without designating or signifying the simultaneous contents, which are formalized in a different way? Signs are not signs of a thing; they are signs of deterritorialization and reterritorialization, they mark a certain threshold crossed in the course of these movements ...
>
> Next, if we consider regimes of signs using this restrictive definition, we see that they are not, or not necessarily, signifiers. Just as signs designate only a certain formalization of expression ... significance itself designates only one specific regime among a number of regimes existing in that particular formalization.
>
> In any case, content and expression are never reducible to signified-signifier ... Expression can never be made into a form reflecting content.
>
> (Deleuze and Guattari, 2004, pp. 75–76)

Here Deleuze and Guattari argue that the relationship between sign and signification is also characterized by multiplicity. Sign-signification is therefore a matter of exterior relations to the assemblage that territorializes or deterritorializes the signification and, thus, to explain the sign-signification relationship, it is important to understand that signification is constituted by the regime of signs. This is interesting in relation to the analysis in this book, because accounting information is perceived as formalized expressions. But as Deleuze and Guattari

(2004, p. 123) note, the formalization in itself is not enough to understand its signification:

> One can proceed as though the formalization of expression were autonomous and self sufficient. Even if that is done, there is such diversity in the forms of expression, such a mixture of these forms, that it is impossible to attach any particular privilege to the form or regime of the "signifier."
>
> (Deleuze and Guattarí, 2004, p. 123)

The complication of understanding signs as signifiers of a thing is based in the argument of difference and repetition, where difference is inherent in chains of repetitions. The signs are therefore "signs of signs" (Deleuze & Guattarí, 2004, p. 124). Thus, the signifying regime is the semiotic that constructs signification of meaning. But this signification, as mentioned in the quotes, is only one signification among others (constituted by other regimes of signs). Thus, several regimes of signs can decode the sign and construct a signification of it. The formalization of information is therefore not enough to understand its signification. Because of the chains of repetitions, the signs are signs of signs (of assemblages of multiplicities); there is therefore not "one" meaning of the sign, no essence. Thus, epistemological objectivity, which is about following the right formalization (procedure) in constructing accounting information, does not resolve the problem of how the sign (of accounting information) is decoded, because it does not refer to a 'thing' or essence but to continuous territorializations and deterritorializations.

This idea is consistent with recent work on connecting organizing and accounting. For instance, Miller and Power (2013) argue that accounting is never just applied to an organizational activity; rather, it must be understood as constituting a calculable space of such activities (see also Lennon, 2019), which they term a 'territorializing' move. Although not building on Deleuze, the work of Miller and Power resembles some aspects of Deleuzoguattarian theory, and their concepts of territorializing may be further developed by incorporating Deleuze and Guattarí's theory. Indeed, accounting territorializes also in a Deleuzian sense. As Neu et al. (2009) write, "technologies such as accounting, and discourses such as accountability come to claim or 'territorialize' particular physical and discursive spaces" (p. 320), and "the first concrete rule for assemblages is to discover what territoriality they envelope" (Deleuze & Guattarí, 1987, pp. 503, 505, 504). Neu et al. (2009, p. 323) suggest that "every social space will be formed differently because of the way that the configuration of assemblages comes together and interacts". Thus, assemblages (including those in accounting) create territories and social spaces, but these territories and social spaces are at all times in a state of flux.

Signifying regime and lines of flight

Significations and counter-significations create a space for possible conflicts. Different regimes of signs create different significations and thus the possibility of conflict. The reason is that counter-significations potentially embody deterritorializations of the signifying regime – potential lines of destruction of the signifying regime. When other significations emerge, the signifying regime must therefore respond to that.

> It incarnates that line of flight the signifying regime cannot tolerate, in other words, an absolute deterritorialization; the regime must block a line of this kind or define it in an entirely negative fashion precisely because it exceeds the degree of deterritorialization of the signifying sign, however high it may be ... Anything that threatens to put the system to flight will be killed or put to flight itself. Anything that exceeds the excess of the signifier or passes beneath it will be marked with a negative value.
>
> (Deleuze & Guattari, 2004, pp. 128–129)

Thus, as we see in the quote, the signifying regime is challenged by other significations. Significations that deterritorialize the signifying regime to a degree that it cannot tolerate (absolute deterritorialization of the signifying regime) will be considered negative and will be pushed toward annihilation (killed) if possible because it "threatens to put the system to flight", in Deleuze and Guattari's (2004, p. 116) own words.

Thus, the concept of signifying can be used to understand how accounting technologies, and their significance and performance, are not only a matter of the technology's materiality but, in a broader perspective, also a matter of the multiplicities running through them and signifying them in a certain way. This again challenges, through deterritorializing, the movement of the signifying regime.

Significations and counter-significations of accounting information, therefore, construct space for conflict about the meaning of the sign (the information), where the obvious line of flight is not obvious and constructs surprising becomings of accounting.

References

Bidima, J.-G., & Warren, N. D. (2005). Philosophy and Literature in Francophone Africa. In K. Wiredu (Ed.), *A Companion to African Philosophy* (549–558). Blackwell Publishing (onlinelibrary.wiley.com, retrieved 25 February 2020).

Chua, W. F. (1986). Radical developments in accounting thought. *Accounting Review, 61*(4), 601.

Chua, W. F. (1995). Experts, networks and inscriptions in the fabrication of accounting images: A story of the representation of three public hospitals. *Accounting, Organizations and Society, 20*(2/3), 111–145.

DeLanda, M. (2006). *A New Philosophy of Society.* London and New York: Continuum International Publishing Group.

Deleuze, G. (2004). *Difference and Repetition.* New York, NY: Continuum.

Deleuze, G., & Guattarí, F. (2004). *A Thousand Plateaus.* New York, NY: Continuum.

Heywood, I. (2002). Deleuze on Francis Bacon. In P. Smith & C. Wilde (Eds.), *A Companion to Art Theory*: Blackwell Publishing (onlinelibrary.wiley. com, Retrieved 25 February 2020).

Hopwood, A. (1978). Towards an organizational perspective for the study of accounting and information systems. *Accounting, Organizations and Society, 3*(1), 3–13.

Hopwood, A. G. (1983). On trying to study accounting in the contexts in which it operates. *Accounting, Organizations and Society, 8*(2/3), 287–305.

Klein, H. K., & Kleinman, D. L. (2002). The social construction of technology: Structural considerations. *Science, Technology, & Human Values, 27*(1), 28–52.

Latour, B. (1987). *Science in Action.* Cambridge, MA: Harvard University Press.

Latour, B. (2005). *Reassembling the Social: An Introduction to Actor-Network-Theory.* Hampshire: Oxford University Press.

Lennon, N. J. (2019). Responsibility accounting, managerial action and 'a counter-ability': Relating the physical and virtual spaces of decision-making. *Scandinavian Journal of Management, 35*(3), 101062.

Martinez, D. E. (2011). Beyond disciplinary enclosures: Management control in the society of control. *Critical Perspectives on Accounting, 22*(2), 200–211.

Martinez, D., & Cooper, D. (2017). Assembling international development: Accountability and the disarticulation of a social movement. *Accounting, Organizations and Society, 63*, 6–20. doi: 10.1016/j.aos.2017.02.002

Meyer, U., & Schulz-Schaeffer, I. (2006). Three forms of interpretive flexibility. *Science, Technology & Innovation Studies, Special Issue 1*(1), 25–40.

Miller, P., & Oleary, T. (1987). Accounting and the construction of the governable person. *Accounting Organizations and Society, 12*(3), 235–265.

Miller, P., & Power, M. (2013). Accounting, organizing, and economizing: Connecting accounting research and organization theory. *The Academy of Management Annals, 7*(1), 557–605.

Miller, P., & Rose, N. (1990). Governing economic life. *Economy and Society, 19*(1), 1–31.

Mouritsen, J., & Bekke, A. (1997). Continuity and discontinuity in accounting technology in Danish state institutions. *Financial Accountability & Management, 13*(2), 165–180.

Neu, D., Everett, J., & Rahaman, A. S. (2009). Accounting assemblages, desire, and the body without organs: A case study of international development lending in Latin America. *Accounting, Auditing & Accountability Journal, 22*(3), 319–350.

Preston, A. M., Cooper, D. J., & Coombs, R. W. (1992). Fabricating budgets: A study of the production of management budgeting in the national health service. *Accounting, Organizations and Society, 17*(6), 561–593.

Robson, K. (1991). On the arenas of accounting change: The process of translation. *Accounting, Organizations and Society, 16*(5–6), 547–570.

Robson, K. (1992). Accounting numbers as "inscription": Action at a distance and the development of accounting. *Accounting, Organizations and Society, 17*(7), 685–708.

3 Is accounting representation work or visualization (re-presentation) work?

The purpose of this chapter is to describe some of the theoretical and historical underpinnings of our argument that conventional accounting theory is, among other things, a theory of representation. In the 1960s, accounting texts articulated an understanding of accounting as representation. This influenced the work on qualitative characteristics of accounting that emerged in the 1970s, when one of the major accounting institutions, the Financial Accounting Standards Board (FASB), started to develop a framework of accounting qualities. We examine the qualitative characteristics of accounting and the theories applied in its development. The first financial accounting standard (FAS) were published by FASB in 1973 (FAS 1).[1]

The FASB

In 1973 Burton published an article with the title 'Some general and specific thoughts on the accounting environment'. This paper is interesting because of Burton's appointment as chief accountant at the United States (US) Securities and Exchange Commission (SEC), an institution closely collaborating with the Accounting Principles Board (APB) and later FASB (Burton, 1973). This paper came out the same year as the FASB was established as the US accounting standards setting body. FASB replaced the APB in 1973, which, according to Burton, was an improvement of the standards of accounting measurements.[2]

The work of FASB materialized in the first statement (FAS 1) in 1973. The title of FAS 1 was 'Disclosure of Foreign Currency Translation Information' (2011). As the title indicates, this first statement did not directly engage with accounting qualities. The only indication about qualities of accounting was its emphasis of accounting for foreign currency as "translation practices to facilitate assessment of possible implications with respect to its financial position and results of operations" (paragraph four). Thus, this paragraph articulates that accounting for foreign currency translation is a representational activity of converting foreign currency assets into the reporting currency, thus representing the current economic state of affairs in an unambiguous manner.

Before FASB issued its fifth statement 'Accounting for Contingencies' in March 1975 (FASB, 1975), none of the prior statements had explicitly dealt with representativeness. But in the fifth statement, they came closer to an idea of accounting as representation, when FASB introduced contingencies into financial reporting. A contingency was defined as "an existing condition, situation, or set of circumstances involving uncertainty as to possible gain or loss to an enterprise that will ultimately be resolved when one or more future events occur or fail to occur" (FASB, 1975). The introduction of an uncertainty element manifested around three possible scenarios of the likelihood of a future event (or set of events) happening – probable, reasonably possible and remote – each representing the likelihood of the occurrence of the event with probable as the most likely and remote as the least likely. The idea of the statement was to make companies disclose loss contingencies as accruals.

Thus, FAS 5 touches the edge of an ideal of representativeness, although without mentioning it directly. The ideal unfolded here is the same as in FAS 1: to strive to make the representation as good as possible, that is, to minimize the difference between representation (the accounting value) and the referent (the event). FASB also discussed this by aligning a claim of integrity of financial statements; if the event was not probable (referring to the three scenarios) and the amount could not be reasonably estimated, then the recognition would erode the integrity of the statement (FASB, 1975, p. 22). Thus, there was an implicit idea about accounting as representation in the text.

Parallel to the publication of FAS, FASB also published a number of concept standards (SFACs).[3] The accounting qualities debate emerged in this work developing the SFACs. The intention of the concept standards was to set "objectives, qualitative characteristics, and other concepts that guide selection of economic phenomena to be recognized and measured for financial reporting and their display in financial statements or related means of communicating information to those who are interested" (Christensen & Frimor, 2014, p. 230).

The SFACs were meant to work as meta-standards, meaning that they would be guides to FASB's development of accounting principles (FASB, 1978). The first SFAC was issued in November 1978 and titled 'Objectives of Financial Reporting by Business Enterprises'. The statement introduced the quality of usefulness, defined as follows:

> financial reporting should provide information that is useful to present and potential investors and creditors and other users in making rational investment, credit, and similar decisions. The information should be comprehensible to those who have a reasonable understanding of business and economic activities and are willing to study the information with reasonable diligence.
>
> (FASB, 1978, pp. 16–17)

To get a sense of what this means, more work is needed on the qualitative characteristics that make information useful; such information was not included in the first. It only stated that usefulness requires a balancing or trade-off of relevance, reliability and other criteria of accounting information.

Accounting: a system of accountability relationships

Parallel to the FASB publications in the 1970s, Ijiri (1975) published a research book, *Theory of Accounting Measurement.* This was one of the first academic works on accounting theory after the FASB was founded. The preface of this book traces interesting movements in accounting, and Ijiri (1975, p. ix) writes, "Accounting is a system designed to facilitate the smooth functioning of accountability relationships among interested parties". Ijiri's move toward accountability is interesting, because it emphasizes the accountability issue of organizational relationships, which is related to accounting as representation.

Ijiri (1975, p. ix) explains how three parties are involved in the construction of accountability: the accountor (the accountable entity), the accountee (the entity which the accountor is accountable to) and the accountant. The accountor is accountable for their activities and the consequences of those activities for the benefit of the accountee (Ijiri, 1975, p. ix). The accountant's role is, according to Ijiri, to act as a third party in the relationship between the accountor and the accountee. This third party, the accountant, can be a bookkeeper, an auditor or an authoritative body. This is where FASB and other authoritative bodies enter the accountability network.

The purpose of the accountant (the standard setter), according to Ijiri (1975, p. ix), is to "assist the accountor in accounting for his activities and their consequences and, at the same time, provide information to the accountee". For standard setters such as FASB, this implies that their principles are important both on a firm level and on a societal level. Standard setters have to align their principles in order to make sure the accountor is accountable for his activities and their consequences and they must provide the accountee with this information. Thus, the question then becomes about accounting representation, which represents the underlying activity, and the question of legitimacy of representations is thus a matter of whether the representation represents what it is and not what it is not (Moore, 2007). This is a matter for the accountant (the standard setter) to make sure the principles enabling accounting as a representation represent what it is rather than what it is not.

Ijiri (1975) problematizes this point by stating that performance measurement is a matter of measuring economic performance of the accountor. In order to do so, performance measurement theory suggests that the accountee must set goals that the accountor should work to achieve. Those goals are by definition propositions about the future, and, therefore, the problem is whether accounting representations offer sufficient means for constructing the accountability relationship between the accountor and the accountee.[4] Ijiri (1975) ends this thought, quite simply, by stating that the financial statement is only the top of the iceberg (p. x).

The establishment of an AICPA study group on qualitative characteristics

In the early 1970s, the American Institute of Certified Public Accountants (AICPA) appointed a study group to work on objectives for financial statements. In 1973 their work was finished and published. In their publication, a chapter was dedicated explicitly to qualitative characteristics of accounting (AICPA, 1973, Chapter 10).

The study group's suggestion for qualitative characteristics of reporting consists of the following points: (1) relevance and materiality, (2) form and substance, (3) reliability, (4) freedom from bias, (5) comparability, (6) consistency and (7) understandability (AICPA, 1973, pp. 57–60).

Within the seven characteristics, the link between representation and activity was indirectly mentioned several times, for example, when they stated that substance, rather than form, must govern the reporting. Also, they reflected on the presence of future benefits and whether to include those. The study group argued that 'substantive economic characteristics' must be a matter of future benefits, and not their technical characteristic or form as was commonly associated with propositions about economic benefits at the time.

In addition to substance, they argued that information must be reliable. The point here is, though, that 100 percent accuracy between information and the object cannot be achieved, but reliability, understood as precision of financial information, must generally be high. In this respect, data limitations and possible measurement errors were also suggested to be disclosed to the user (AICPA, 1973, p. 58). These concerns indicate that representation and referent must be closely linked, and further, that they can be closely linked (i.e., that accounting is representation).

Performance measurement criteria

For Ijiri (1975), accountability and performance measurement are closely connected because, in order to be accountable, the accountor must know the goals through which he is accountable to the accountee. He argued for two criteria of performance measures that should ensure the measure is univocal and unambiguous: the criteria of hardness and the criteria of objectivity.

Hardness: The hardness of a measure refers to the ambiguity of a measure. As Ijiri (1975, p. 36) explains, "a 'hard' measure is one constructed in such a way that it is difficult for people to disagree. A 'soft' measure is one that can easily be pushed in one direction or the other". As an example, cash balance is a hard measure, but goodwill is a soft measure because of the reliability of the measure. A highly reliable, unambiguous measure is hard, and an unreliable, ambiguous measure is soft. But the measure itself is not the only defining feature of hardness. The process of constructing the measure, the transformation from object to number, is important too. If this process is verifiable, the hardness of the measure is higher. Ijiri (1975, p. 36) therefore writes that calculating the measure should be carried out by following a calculative method that makes the measure reliable; this point refers to the rigidity of the calculation.

Objectivity: According to Ijiri (1975), objectivity in accounting measurement does not mean that the representation refers to an 'existing external reality'.[5] His ontological position in terms of discussing objectivity is that "we may accept, at least for the sake of the argument, that there is a reality outside the mind" (Ijiri, 1975, p. 36, paraphrased). However, the discussion of objectivity becomes problematic because of the meta-theoretical problem of whether there are more objective accounting numbers (perhaps exogenous to the accounting calculation) waiting to be discovered by accountants, or whether the accounting calculations construct the numbers in themselves (endogenously).

Ijiri (1975, p. 37) realizes this issue and argues, therefore, that objectivity must be a matter of consensus among "the persons who perceive the object in question". This means that the value of the firm is considered to be objective if there is consensus among the values. But, obviously, this is potentially problematic because the value of the firm is by definition a subjective measure where the value depends on the assumptions made in the valuation method. To test the objectivity of a measure, Ijiri suggests, as a working condition, to ask a group of measurers to measure the same object. After each person has assigned a value to the object, it becomes possible to calculate the variance of the values. If the variance is low, close to zero, Ijiri argues that the objectivity of the measure increases. However, this implies that objectivity is a matter of standardizing assumptions and calculative methods (because by doing so and making people follow these methods the variance will decrease), but the relations between assumptions and reality is actually not discussed here.

Ijiri also borrows the AICPA study group's criterion 'freedom from bias' to extend the perspective of objectivity. The idea is that the measurers, who agree on the value of an object, must be independent from each other. Where objectivity is argued to be a reasonable criterion for external reporting, it might not be suitable in situations where people have different interests. In such situations, Ijiri argues, the criterion of hardness suits much better, because it eliminates the possibility of questioning the valuation. The reason is that the 'freedom from bias' criterion cannot be satisfied in such situations because of the assumption of opportunism; people act in self-interest seeking ways (Williamson, 1985).

Ijiri's discussion of identifiability, through the theoretical concepts of surrogate and principal, is interesting for the representativeness of accounting. A surrogate is a thing used to "convey information about the state of something else" (Ijiri, 1975, p. 40), and the principal is the thing, or phenomenon, represented by the surrogate. Ijiri explains the surrogate-principal relationship as a relationship of representation:

> A surrogate is related to a principal by means of a rule of representation. If P is a set of all varieties that the principal can assume and S is a set of all varieties that the surrogate can assume, then the representation rule is considered a function that maps P into S.
>
> (Ijiri, 1975, p. 40)

This representation rule underlines a unidirectional relationship between the principal and the surrogate. As Ijiri (1975, p. 41) describes,

> identifiability is the most crucial quality for a surrogate to have ... A surrogate without identifiability is ... like a clock that does not keep time or a car that does not run. These items may still be useful in some respect but certainly not for their intended purposes.

Here, Ijiri is making a direct point about representativity of accounting; namely that accounting is a process of representation (representing other underlying affairs).

Qualitative characteristics in SFAC no. 2

FASB (1980a) published its second SFAC in 1980. The second SFAC is an extension of the discussion on qualitative characteristics of accounting in the first SFAC. The focal point of the conceptual statement is not financial reporting in general, as it was in the first SFAC. The focus was on accounting information. The scope of the standard is, therefore, narrower than its predecessor.

The second SFAC is interesting because it discusses some of the same qualitative characteristics as found by Ijiri (1975) and the publication from AICPA's study group from 1973. But this statement takes a step further and contains a hierarchy of accounting qualities starting with 'usefulness' at the top, which was the central part of the first SFAC. The next most important quality is understandability because, as FASB argues, the information provided is of no use if the user cannot understand it. For this reason, usefulness and, following that, understandability are qualities that precede the more interior qualities of the information itself.

The next level in the hierarchy refers to decision-specific qualities. Relevance and reliability are the most important qualities here, because they qualify information as useful or not (FASB, 1980a). Relevance is defined as timely information and predictability value and/or feedback value. Reliability is defined as information, which is a faithful representation, verifiable and neutral (FASB, 1980a).

This discussion on relevance expresses an important assumption regarding the connection between information (representation) and the past and the future (reality). First of all, relevance is defined as information that "can make a difference to decisions by improving decision makers' capacities to predict or by providing feedback on earlier expectations" (FSAB, 1980a, p. 5), but, perhaps more importantly, "knowledge about the outcomes of actions already taken will generally improve decision makers' abilities to predict the results of similar future actions. Without a knowledge of the past, the basis for a prediction will usually be lacking". The interesting point here is the idea of similarity as a necessity of predictability; if the future is similar to the past, then information about the past will have predictable value. But this also means that information built on past events is relevant only to the extent that the future is similar to the past.

Representativeness

As mentioned, reliability in the second SFAC is conceptualized as representational faithfulness, neutrality and verifiability. Representational faithfulness indicates a representational ideal of accounting – accounting ought to represent something. Representational faithfulness is a new term introduced in the second SFAC and is not found in any of the previous books or papers on qualitative characteristics of accounting. It is related to the AICPA study group's discussion of reliability; however, it is more precisely defined in this statement:

> The reliability of a measure rests on the faithfulness with which it represents what it purports to represent, coupled with an assurance for the user that it has that representational quality ... Reliability rests upon the extent to which the accounting description or measurement is verifiable and representationally faithful ... Representational Faithfulness (means) correspondence or agreement between a measure or description and the phenomenon that it purports to represent (sometimes called validity).
>
> (FASB, 1980a, pp. 6 and 10)

The second SFAC claims that the characteristics that distinguish better information from inferior information are primarily relevance and reliability (FASB, 1980a, p. 14). FASB touches on the problem of representation and referent by discussing cartography as a metaphor for accounting. In their depiction, the information is the map and the accountant is the cartographer. FASB, however, claims that it is problematic to design a 'general-purpose' map that aims to satisfy all user needs. Such a map will be ineffective because the cartographer (the accountant) must make choices about which information to include.

Representational faithfulness

FASB argues that accounting decisions are always imbued with the tension between relevance and reliability, meaning that an increase in relevance will imply a decrease in reliability and vice versa (FASB, 1980a). Reliability is discussed through a metaphor of drugs. Drugs can be reliable by curing what they claim to cure or when the label on the drug corresponds to the content in the drug. Reliability in the second SFAC is defined as the latter: the label of the accounting information must correspond to its content. To stress this point, FASB introduced the notion of representational faithfulness, defined as follows: "Representational faithfulness means correspondence or agreement between a measure or description and the phenomenon it purports to represent". (FASB, 1980a, p. 28).

However, this definition leads to a new problem, namely what it means to represent what it purports to represent. The second SFAC expresses this through a simple example of the costs of acquiring assets: if the inventory consists only of good A and good A is bought three times during January in quantities 10, 13 and 16 at the prices DKK 105, DKK 120 and DKK 113, and the company gets a discount of ten percent for each piece more than 20 they buy each month (which means that they get a ten percent discount on the last 19 pieces), how can we know what the cost of each good is?

The first ten products are easy to value; they cost DKK 10 each. But what about piece numbered 11, 12, 13 or even worse, piece number 21? Depending on how the registrations happen, it is possible to calculate the value of each product (e.g., fist-in-first-out (FIFO) and average prices). But, if the last 16 pieces were bought to obtain a bonus when a certain amount of products are bought, the accountant must make a choice about how to account for the purchasing politic and bonus arrangements in the cost estimates.

This example is a very simple problematization of representational faithfulness. In reality, when manufacturing cost calculations are made, depreciations and estimates of future values (e.g., market values of assets) will challenge the link between representation and referent even more. Valuation of assets can give an example of this: an asset can only be recorded when it expresses a value to the owner. But this value, independent of whether it is recorded at historical costs, market value or depreciated costs, relies on some conditions about the future. If the asset has a value in the future, the asset book value could be a faithful representation of that value. But the faithfulness thus relies on the assumption that the asset value represents this future value that, for example, a buyer is willing to pay for it. Therefore, if a balance sheet item on the asset side should represent the value a company has, the valuation of the asset must be a projection of the future value in order to be reliable. This means that both market values and historical costs can be faithful only to the extent that the proposition about future value is true, as long as they are included on the balance sheet's asset side.

The problem is therefore whether cost calculations as valuations of assets express faithfully the future value of the asset (FASB, 1980a, 1980b). This is not a simple problem; it is a matter of making choices about how to calculate it, which numbers to include in the valuation and when then asset value is planned to be realized.

Related to this problem of representativeness, the second SFAC also discusses the relation between reliability and predictability. It states, "Reliability as a quality of a predictor has a somewhat different meaning from reliability as a quality of a measure" (FASB, 1980a, paragraph 75). FASB addresses this point very precisely by stating that accounting reliability should be judged not by its predictability of the future, but, oppositely, on the relation between representation and referent. Since predictability depends on various other factors, for example, the forecasting model applied (denoted as the 'predictive model' in the second SFAC), the information's quality of reliability is very much a matter of the subjective choices of the accountants.

IASC's work on representational faithfulness

In the late 1980s, the International Accounting Standards Committee (IASC) published a framework very similar to the one FASB made.[6] In the IASC's framework, the qualitative characteristics developed to measure usefulness in accounting information are understandability, relevance, reliability and comparability.[7] IASC also adopted FASB's concept of representational faithfulness in its operationalization of reliability. Reliability was defined as follows: "Information has the quality of reliability when it is free from material error and bias and can be depended upon by users to represent faithfully that which it either purports to represent or could reasonably be expected to represent" (IASB, 2007).

Two differences in the definition are evident when comparing this to the second SFAC. First, the SFAC states that, in order to be reliable, the representation must be coupled with an assurance for the user that emphasizes the information's 'representational quality'. The second difference is that the IASC framework not only argues that the information must represent what it purports to represent, but specifies that it should represent what it 'could reasonably be expected to represent'. This specification may have been included in the definition to allow IASC to record discounted cash flow (DCF) valuations in the balance sheet. Furthermore, in FASB's second SFAC, this is denoted representational faithfulness, whereas in the IASC framework, it is defined as faithful representation. This difference in terminology could be to stress faithful representation as a quality of the activity of representing, which concerns the process of representing, and not leaving the criteria as quality of the end product – the representation. This argument is partially confirmed in the IASC framework when it emphasizes the process rather than the product.

Even though there are slight differences between the SFAC standards and the IASC framework, they are still founded on the same representational basis that representation and referent can be reliably linked.

Qualitative characteristics of accounting

As we have seen, the work of the financial institutions on accounting qualities and representational faithfulness articulates an understanding of accounting information as the process of representing. However, within the literature it is difficult to obtain an understanding of what it explicitly means to represent faithfully. It seems to be that both IASB and FASB acknowledge the difficulty of accounting representation; they do not specifically talk about accounting information as representing an 'underlying economic reality', or underlying truth. In contrast, they emphasize process. Instead of representing some underlying reality, representational faithfulness must be about reporting according to given standards. In this way, it becomes an epistemological, or procedural faithfulness, more than an ontological faithfulness. However, the work on accounting qualities strongly articulates a representational ideal, namely that accounting information is constructed to represent something, for example, the idea of surrogate and principal (Ijiri, 1975).

Even though the definition of representational faithfulness is difficult to identify and FASB uses metaphors to give an indication for what it could mean, the notion is repeated within the later frameworks for accounting qualities (e.g., the IASC framework).

In consequence, representational faithfulness seems to be something that standard setters cannot precisely define or conceptualize. This could indicate a problem in terms of the role representativeness plays in accounting information and, in continuation of this, a problem for accountants regarding how to meet the requirement of providing representative information.

This section has set the scene for the representational ideal, as articulated in accounting theory and accounting standards; the next section reviews the debates among researchers about representational faithfulness and the existence of an underlying economic reality, or truth.

Research on faithful representation

Researchers have discussed the representational ideal of accounting since the second SFAC was published in 1980. This section reviews academic articles on the topic of representational faithfulness (and faithful representation).[8] In 1981, Donald Kirk, chairman of FASB, published an article in which he expressed a need for a conceptual framework for standard setters of accounting standards (Kirk & Horngren, 1981). In this article, they argued that the framework was intended to "serve as a system of accountability for the board in fulfilling its public responsibility" (Kirk & Horngren, 1981, p. 83) and to align the individuals within the standard setting bodies to adopt the same perception of 'reality':

> Without a framework, it is difficult for a standard setter to assess the contention that a particular method of accounting better reflects 'economic reality' or is more 'useful' than an alternative method. Reality is personal to the observer: a framework helps identify the particular facet of reality that is most useful and that should be or can be measured in financial statements.
>
> (Kirk and Horngren, 1981, p. 83)

This article raises an important, yet fundamental question, which was why FASB was building a technical framework in the first place. They argued that the reason was due to an axiomatic belief, based on the assumption that "if we only had a foundation, deductive logic would lead us to the correct answer" (Kirk & Horngren, 1981, p. 88).

Vickrey (1985) argued that an analysis of normative information qualities (NIQs), such as the second SFAC framework, should be built on the relation between information system qualities and usefulness on the individual level. From Vickrey's (1985) perspective, information system qualities must meet the criteria of normativity only to the extent that they are useful on the level of the individual. Vickrey (1985) questions representativeness when arguing that it is important to remember that different NIQs, such as the ones FASB developed, lead to different accounting policy decisions.

Vickrey (1985) defines 'normative' as "qualities which are individually necessary and collectively sufficient for usefulness in probability revision in the context of expected utility maximization". The focus here is on utility maximization in economic decision-making. The article questions the purpose of a framework (of accounting qualities), similar to that of Kirk and Horngren (1981). But where they later discuss purpose and social choice between constituencies, Vickrey (1985) focuses on the qualitative framework and is thus not considering the social aspect of its constitution.

In 1986, David Solomons (1986a) published an evaluation of the conceptual framework. Although he argues against the skepticism about the need for a conceptual framework, he acknowledges skepticism about the outcome of the project (which had then been running for nine years).

Solomons (1986a, p. 121) does not explicitly evaluate on the second, but a text box on representational faithfulness in the paper shows, as an example, how actuarials' many assumptions about the future are challenging representational faithfulness because "some or all of these assumptions will prove not to be in accordance with the way things turn out". Solomons (1986a, p. 121) states that the outcome of the conceptual framework is very weak, and he even calls it 'a lost opportunity'. This standpoint is summed up in the very last paragraph of the paper where he states that

> A 'guiding model of the overall order', a 'utopia', a 'guiding conception of an internally consistent model' – this is what the conceptual framework might have been. In my judgment the result of the board's work falls dismally short of this ideal.

Thus, as we can see, some believe accounting can produce 'faithful representation', while others are much more skeptical because, essentially, the reification of accounting numbers relies on many subjective decisions and propositions, for example, regarding future values and future depreciations (life expectancy of assets).

The 'reality' accounting represents

Parallel to this paper, Solomons (1986b) also published a book with the title *Making Accounting Policy*, in which Chapter 5 is devoted to the second SFAC. Here, Solomons explains the inherent problem with the notion of 'economic reality' where accountants strive "to present a picture of economic reality in an enterprise's financial statements", but where "economic reality ... is incapable of precise definition" (p. 92). Again, Solomons (1986b, p. 93) relates the notion of representational faithfulness to pensions: "virtually none of the factors that determine the ultimate cost of a pension plan to an employer can be foreseen accurately during the working lives of the employees covered by a plan". This illustrates the problem of economic reality and estimates about the future; if the cost components cannot be foreseen accurately, how can a cost estimate then represent an 'economic reality'?

This relationship between accounting numbers and reality is also discussed in Ruth Hines's 1988 paper with the intriguing title 'Financial Accounting: In Communicating Reality, We Construct Reality'. The interesting point in this paper is the argument about what an organization is (and the boundaries that define what it is not). Hines problematizes the point of realization, especially in terms of goodwill. She argues that financial matters become real only to the extent that they are realized. Hines argues that, in practice, the point of realization is not related to a certain event that is realized, but, rather, it is related to a calculative decision of realizing the matter.

She relates this to financial accounting and argues that nobody really knows what 'the full picture' is, and therefore, the notion of "a true, a fair view of something – depends on people deciding that they have the full picture" (Hines, 1988, p. 252). The same goes for faithful representation. Faithful representation in accounting assumes that we know what the 'right representation' is. Thus, the ideal of representing a so-called real underlying economic reality is rejected.

Hines published another, related, article in 1991. In this paper, she explores the significance of standard setting or setters in the construction of reality. The article focuses explicitly on the problematic relationship between financial accounting and the 'economic reality'. Hines argues that the logic of faithful representation and the consequences of this logic for conceptually prescriptive accounting models covers all accounting theory: "As pointed out previously, the FASB's CF reflects the reasoning of members of the accounting profession, and industry, and user groups. It is a process of reasoning, maintaining the assumption of an objective, intersubjective world as central" (Hines, 1991, p. 319). Thus, the idea of having an objective reality is becoming an ontology in the accounting profession, even though nobody seems to be able to describe what representation means (or *what* is represented). Hines argues that, for some reason, the standard setters take for granted that it is possible to represent faithfully (that there is a referent to which the representation is a surrogate). She compares this ontological belief of the accounting profession, including the standard setters, to the Azande tribe in Africa whose members 'know that an oracle exists' and for this reason do not question the oracle's existence at all (Hines, 1991).

Hines's ontological problematization of representational faithfulness resonates in several other research articles as well. For example, Ingram and Rayburn (1989) argue that accounting reports are distortions of reality and that "accounting reports are not maps of reality, because there is no empirical referent for much of the information contained in accounting reports". The 'truth' of accounting reports is, for this reason, considered to be a "subjective understanding to be manufactured and agreed upon" (Ingram & Rayburn, 1989, p. 59).

In the 1990s, the discussion of accounting qualities continued. In 1991, Solomons (1991a) wrote a critique of the work of Tinker (1985). Tinker (1991) responded to this by arguing that ideals such as representational faithfulness are epistemological standards rather than ontological standards, because they are reasonable only within the epistemic position in which they are created. Solomons (1991b) responded by stating that both he and Tinker agree on the point that accounting representations are socially constructed. However, Solomons reproduces his previous standpoint when he states that society needs ideals, such as representational faithfulness and other qualitative characteristics to assess accounting standards, exactly because accounting is a social construct.

Kripke (1989) initiated a discussion regarding conceptual frameworks in 'Reflections on the FASB's Conceptual Framework for Accounting and on Auditing'. He argued that FASB failed to do a good job when they developed the framework: "in my opinion, the Board's earnest effort has failed" (Kripke, 1989, p. 11). The critique is directed to the internal consistency between standards and conceptual standards, and, as an example, Kripke applies representational faithfulness to the definition of an asset in the third SFAC and concludes that an asset is defined as follows: "a probable future benefit that involves a capacity ... to contribute directly or indirectly to future net cash inflows" (Kripke, 1989, p. 15). Hence, it is inaccurate from a representational faithfulness point of view to measure assets on a cost basis when they are defined as future value in the third SFAC (FASB, 1980b).

Kripke's work criticizes the FASB's conceptual framework on the grounds that the standards are inconsistent and that the qualities are contradictory (relevance/verifiability/reliability). He concludes that a framework like FASB's is confusing both for accountants and for auditors. His recommendation is that the FASB should appoint an overriding quality of accounting information, which should be representational faithfulness. This could qualify the auditor opinion that "representational faithfulness to the events and results of the period on which the opinion is expressed" (Kripke, 1989, p. 65). By doing so, the auditor would be able to "conclude that the set of financial statements adequately mirrors the economic activity it reports" (Kripke, 1989, p. 65, quotation marks removed). In this way, Kripke actually articulates the ontology criticized by Hines, that accounting information has representational qualities and represents something (here 'economic activity').

Kripke's article was debated in three subsequent articles, written by Ronen and Sorter, Burton and Kirk. Even though Ronen and Sorter (1989) argue that Kripke's critique is 'fair and constructive', they disagree with his conclusion that accounting "should be aimed toward becoming consistently useful and representationally faithful". They find consistency and representational faithfulness to be wrong ideals and argue that such ideals require logical analysis based on the definitions of the ideals. They take the critique seriously but argue, parallel with David Solomons, that a board such as FASB must strive toward a framework that represents faithfully the economic reality, rather than considering game theoretic self-interest optimums.

Burton's (1989) response to Kripke is mainly aimed at Kripke's solution in which he proposes a pragmatic approach to standard setting "driven by the underlying principles of consistency, representational faithfulness, and usefulness" (Burton, 1989, p. 79).[9]

The last response to Kripke's article was written by Kirk (1989). It is not surprising that he, as the former chairman of FASB, defends the need for a framework to "point the user of the framework in a direction generally believed to be in the best interests of the public" (Kirk, 1989, p. 85). Kirk writes that Kripke's suggestion of a pragmatic approach to standard setting is useless in practice because of the lack of definitions of core elements of consistency, representational faithfulness and usefulness. His concluding claim is that the reconceptualization proposed by Kripke is unnecessary. In the dialogue between Kripke and Kirk, Kirk states that FASB purposefully left the notion of economic reality out of the definition of representational faithfulness in the 1980 framework because 'economic reality' is an abstract term that would not benefit the standard setting work, because it gives space to a discussion about what the economic reality actually is.

This is interesting because this signifies a change from a principle of conformity with economic reality to a less clear phrase, namely that accounting should represent 'what it purports to represent'. The description of the FASB framework shows that this also changed the ideal of representational faithfulness from being a matter of coherence between representation and referent, where the referent used to be the 'economic reality', to one about representing what the 'label' of the representation states (the metaphor of the label on the drug). This means that historical cost can be a faithful representation if the representation states that it represents historical costs.

Therefore, representational faithfulness changes to become a matter of being explicit about the standards with which accounting calculations comply, that is, its 'label'. Thus, representational faithfulness changes to express an epistemological or procedural faithfulness, rather than an ontological faithfulness. Nonetheless, the ideal of representativeness is still articulated; the information is still meant to represent something; therefore, it must act as a surrogate of a principle.

Bushman and Indjejikian (1993) are also interested in representational faithfulness and suggest that distorted accounting information (unfaithful representations) can be beneficial when they are used for stewardship. This point is contradictory to the idea that it is reasonable to construct a set of qualitative criteria for 'useful accounting information' that applies to a broad set of accounting purposes, which the acknowledgment of FAS as social constructions from the social constructivism perspective would also claim. Bushman and Indjejikian (1993) unfold their argument in a compensation scheme context where compensation contracts are used in multitasking settings (p. 766 for an elaboration). Performance is measured on aggregate performance measures. In this setting, Bushman and Indjejikian (1993) show that biased measures can be used strategically for other purposes, such as stewardship. For this reason, the paper shows that a general-purpose framework meant to cover both stewardship and economic decision-making can hardly be obtained, as it then serves different, contradictory purposes.

Gibbins and Willett (1997) also contribute to theorizing representational faithfulness. They raise a question about what accounting numbers represent (related to the wealth-creating activities of firms). Their point is critical, and they argue that accounting data is a sociotechnical construct from "an underlying data generating system that defines the statistical character of the resulting data" (Gibbins and Willett, 1997, p. 128). They argue that the accounting system is the back end of the financial reports. In their view, this acts as a layer, a disclosure filter, that is put on the measurement of economic events. This is a problem for the assumption of a direct relationship between reference and referent. Gibbins and Willett (1997) give several examples of how the representation becomes unfaithful because of the way transactions are recorded. In addition, the choice of measurement, for example, stock movement at LIFO, FIFO or average costs, gives the number statistical properties which arguably contradicts the principle of faithful representation. In this way, they argue that the link between registration, measurement and the underlying economic event is essential for how faithful a representation can be.

More recent developments in qualitative characteristics of accounting

In 2010, IASB published a new version of the conceptual framework (IASB, 2010). In this work, the notion of faithful representation substitutes its previous principle of 'reliability', and the qualitative trade-off is now between relevance and faithful representation. The reason for doing this is that faithful representation is considered to be what the conceptual framework has meant when referring to reliability, that it represents what it purports to represent (IASB, 2010, paragraphs QC12 and BC3.19). Faithful representation is conceptualized as a representation that is complete, neutral and free from bias.[10]

In the definition of completeness, the epistemological or procedural faithfulness is even more strongly articulated. The framework states

> a complete depiction of a group of assets would include, at a minimum, a description of the nature of the assets in the group, a numerical depiction of all of the assets in the group, and a description of what the numerical depiction represents (for example, original cost, adjusted cost or fair value).
>
> (IASB, 2010, paragraph QC13)

The framework describes how the completeness criteria would also sometimes require a description of "factors and circumstances that might affect their quality and nature, and the process used to determine the numerical depiction". This means that if certain things are known to potentially affect the asset's value, they should be described. The conceptual framework also explains how accounting estimates can be considered to be faithful representations (IASB, 2010, paragraph QC15). Here, the emphasis on disclosing procedure is also evident as a condition for being faithful. This means that "unfaithful" estimates are not a matter of their composition but a matter of whether the estimation process is explained or not. This is based on the idea that estimates cannot be said to be accurate or inaccurate, due to their very nature as estimates.

The text in the 2010 framework avoids the notion of underlying economic reality. Later in the framework, faithful representation is defined as "the faithful depiction in financial reports of economic phenomena" (IASB, 2010, paragraph BC3.24). The choice of the word 'depiction' could be random, but it could also indicate that the framework takes a step away from the ideal of representativeness and thus acknowledges that accounting figures do not represent something underlying, but they are (social) constructions that are manufactured or produced to present the economic phenomenon rather than representing it (an example could be how transfer pricing decisions redistribute costs and revenue between subsidiaries or associated companies). This leads to the principle of disclosing the calculative procedure as the turning point of representing faithfully.

The review of the literature on representation in accounting in this chapter therefore shows how the representational ideal has changed from an ontological concern in the 1960s to a more social, epistemological concern today. And, so far, the solution to the problem of representing faithfully is to disclose the calculative procedure behind the numbers rather than representing the exact correct number itself.

Summing up

Early research from the 1970s and onward, starting with the work of FASB and Ijiri (1975), is concerned with the usefulness of accounting information. The literature on qualitative characteristics, especially representational faithfulness, is ambiguous and does not offer a consistent definition of what accounting representations are faithful to. It must represent 'what it purports to represent' (FASB, 1980a). Some argue that it is about representing an underlying economic truth, while others claim that it is about following procedures and being faithful to the way accounting information, in the financial reports, is described and calculated (this implies that historical costs versus fair value is not a matter of representing a more 'true' economic reality by choosing one over the other, but rather a matter of specifying how the value is calculated). Others again criticize the entire stream of literature on the 'representational ideal', by stating that qualitative accounting characteristics are not suitable to address what accounting is and does, and therefore, the standard setting bodies should see their role and responsibility in society much broader than they do today.

This is a meta-theoretical concern; rather than being ontologically representational faithful, accounting has moved toward an ideal of epistemological representational faithfulness. This means, first, rather than being faithful to 'the world' (or the economic reality), representational faithfulness has come to mean being faithful to the accounting standards themselves. Second, it makes it difficult in standard setting to use representational faithfulness as a quality by which new standards and amendments to existing standards are based upon, since the concept has moved away from the ideal of representing an objective 'reality'. The concept is not precisely conceptualized in the literature, and, as argued, the lack of consensus on what the representation ought to represent faithfully is a potential problem for accounting practitioners as well as accounting setters and researchers.

This point resonates with the ambitions of the standards. One ambition is to represent the phenomena that economic information in financial reports is based upon (otherwise usefulness is compromised), and another ambition is comparability. Comparability is not so much about being an ontologically faithful representation but about being an epistemologically, or procedurally, faithful representation; accountants must be faithful to the standards; otherwise, comparability is compromised.

Nonetheless, this shows that a representational ideal is very strong in the financial accounting literature, especially in the development of accounting qualities. Representational faithfulness, as a conceptual quality, continues in current discussions and is still present in IASB's and FASB's frameworks from 2010 and in the common framework FASB and IASB published together in 2012 (Ernst & Young, 2012). Faithful representation was even moved up in the qualitative hierarchy to substitute for reliability.

However, even though the notion of accounting as representation survives, the 2010 framework articulates the notion of 'depiction' rather than 'representation', which indicates a concern for accounting as constructing (Hines, 1988), rather than representing economic phenomena.

The next chapters study accounting (as representation) from a practice-oriented view, to theorize how accounting works if this does not happen through the work of representing economic phenomena, but rather by constituting a version of reality through numbers. Therefore, the rest of the book describes how accounting produces effects, if the effects are constituted through the process of fabricating accounting numbers in certain forms.

Notes

1 Before this, the Accounting Principles Board (APB) had issued account-ing standards in the US, but it did not deal explicitly with accounting qualities.

2 APB was founded by the American Institute of Certified Public Account-ants (AICPA) and was therefore not independent of AICPA, which could be problematic. FASB was independent and therefore had better struc-tural conditions for succeeding as a standard setter (Burton, 1973).

3 The abbreviation 'SFAC' comes from 'Statements of Financial Account-ing Concepts'.

4 The accountability relationship means 'to account for', which Ijiri (1975) defines as "to explain a consequence (e.g. a cash balance) by providing a set of causes (e.g. cash receipts and disbursements) that have collectively produced the result".

5 The question of whether such a reality exists is a meta-theoretical concern, which Ijiri (1975) does not discuss.

6 In the 1980s, FASB and IASC worked independent of each other. Yet, it looks as if the SFAC framework highly influenced the work on the IASC framework (Hendriksen & Breda, 1992, p. 241).

7 IASC (2007) denotes these 'principal qualitative characteristics'.

8 A discussion of fair value accounting versus historical cost accounting un-folds in the domain of faithful representation, and proponents and oppo-nents of both measurement techniques exist. But as fair value accounting is not explicitly the theme of this paper, the dialogue on issues related to cost recognition is not part of the review.

9 Burton's (1989, p. 81) response is not relevant for this article, because it reflects on the failure of the FASB work and argues the problem to be one of politics, where Burton ends with "While Professor Kripke and I clearly have some differences in detail, I believe we are on the same basic wave-length working toward the same objective".

10 Completeness was discussed in earlier conceptualizations of representa-tional faithfulness, but it is more elaborately described in the 2010 frame-work. In 1980, completeness centered on freedom from bias and that no material necessary to "insure that it validly represents the underlying events and conditions" is left out (FASB, 1980a, paragraph 79).

References

AICPA. (1973). Objectives of Financial Statements: The Study Group on the Objectives of Financial Statements, American Institute of Certified Public Accountants.

Burton, J. C. (1973). Some general and specific thoughts on the accounting environment. *Journal of Accountancy, 136*, 40–46.

Burton, J. C. (1989). A commentary on the reflections of Homer Kripke. *Jour-nal of Accounting, Auditing and Finance, 4*(1), 79–81.

Bushman, R. M., & Indjejikian, R. J. (1993). Stewardship value of "Distorted" accounting disclosures. *The Accounting Review, 68*(4), 765–782.

Christensen, J., & Frimor, H. (2014). Economic Theory of Financial Reporting Regulation. In C. van Mourik & P. Walton (Eds.), *The Routledge Companion to Accounting, Reporting and Regulation* (228–245). New York, NY: Routledge.

Ernst&Young. (2012). International GAAP 2012. Generally Accepted Accounting Practice under International Financial Reporting Standards.: Ernst & Young.

FASB. (1975). Statement of Financial Accounting Standards No. 5. Accounting for Contingencies.: Financial Accounting Standards Board.

FASB. (1978). Statement of Financial Accounting Concepts No. 1. Objectives of Financial Reporting by Business Enterprises: Financial Accounting Standards Board.

FASB. (1980a). Statement of Financial Accounting Concepts No. 2. Qualitative Characteristics of Accounting Information.: Financial Accounting Standards Board.

FASB. (1980b). Statement of Financial Accounting Concepts No. 3. Elements of Financial Statements of Business Enterprises.: Financial Accounting Standards Board.

FASB. (2011). FASB Pre-Codification Standards (http://www.fasb.org/st/): Financial Accounting Standards Board.

Gibbins, M., & Willett, R. J. (1997). New light on accrual, aggregation and allocation, using an axiomatic analysis of accounting numbers' fundamental and statistical character. *ABACUS, 33*(2), 137–167.

Hendriksen, E. S., & Breda, M. F. V. (1992). *Accounting Theory*. Homewood, IL: Irwin.

Hines, R. (1988). Financial accounting: In communicating reality, we construct reality. *Accounting, Organizations and Society, 13*(3), 251–261.

Hines, R. (1991). The FASB's conceptual framework, financial accounting and the maintenance of the social world. *Accounting, Organizations and Society, 16*(4), 313–331.

IASB. (2007). IFRS - A Guide Through International Financial Reporting Standards (IFRSs): IASC Foundation Education.

IASB. (2010). Conceptual Framework for Financial Reporting 2010. London: IFRS Foundation.

Ijiri, Y. (1975). *Theory of Accounting Measurement*. Sarasota: American Accounting Association.

Ingram, R. W., & Rayburn, F. R. (1989). Representational faithfulness and economic consequences. *Journal of Accounting and Public Policy, 8*(1), 57–68.

Kirk, D. J. (1989). Reflections on a "reconceptualization of accounting": A commentary on parts i–iv of Homer Kripke's paper, "Reflections on the FASB's conceptual framework for accounting and on auditing". *Journal of Accounting, Auditing and Finance, 4*(1), 83–105.

Kirk, D. J., & Horngren, C. T. (1981). Statement in quotes. *Journal of Accountancy, 151*(4), 83–95.

Moore, N. (2007). Icons of control: Deleuze, signs, law. *International Journal for the Semiotics of Law, 20*(1), 33–54.

Ronen, J., & Sorter, G. (1989). Reflections on "reflections on the FASB's conceptual framework for accounting and on auditing". *Journal of Accounting, Auditing and Finance, 4*(1), 67–77.

Solomons, D. (1986a). The FASB's conceptual framework: An evaluation. *Journal of Accountancy, 161*(6), 114–124.

Solomons, D. (1986b). *Making Accounting Policy.* Oxford: Oxford University Press.

Solomons, D. (1991a). Accounting and social change: A neutralist view. *Accounting, Organizations and Society, 16*(3), 287–295.

Solomons, D. (1991b). A rejoinder. *Accounting, Organizations and Society, 16*(3), 311–312.

Tinker, T. (1985). *Paper Prophets. A Social Critique of Accounting.* Westport, CT: Praeger Publishers.

Vickrey, D. W. (1985). Normative information qualities: A contrast between information-economics and FASB perspectives. *ABACUS, 21*(2), 115–130.

Williamson, O. E. (1985). *The Economics Institutions of Capitalism Firms, Markets Relational Contracting*: New York, NY: The Free Press.

4 What is accountability? Accountability, responsibility and responsibility accounting

The concept of accountability has been studied from many theoretical points of views such as financial considerations (Ijiri, 1975), ethics (Messner, 2009; Roberts, 2009), management technologies (Kirk & Mouritsen, 1996) and accountability as an everyday practice, with deep roots in the society's construction (Munro, 1996). Another stream of literature describes responsibility accounting as a method to render business unit managers accountable, which requires some level of transparency between the accountor (the accountable entity) and the accountee (the entity which the accountor is accountable to), through the accounts by which the accountor is held accountable (Ijiri, 1975). Responsibility accounting does this by delegating responsibility for a particular part of the budget to a manager in charge of a business unit by, in principle, evaluating one single number (revenue, costs, profit, return on investment and so on). The idea is to hold the manager responsible for the decisions they make in relation to the decision rights that the responsibility center has been assigned. This form of accountability is measured in terms of the decisions' effects on financial numbers (Zimmerman, 2011), thus providing more transparency.

However, in order to provide transparency, accounting numbers must represent the economic conditions, or performance, of the organizational unit that is presented through the numbers. On the organizational side, this is done in responsibility accounting by constructing business units where managers are held responsible for (parts of) the business's finances, as described in the introduction.

Accountability is about giving and receiving accounts of whether individuals meet the responsibility they are assigned. This implies that accountability is concerned with the justification of actions related to the responsibility individuals are assigned. In this way, it relates to hierarchy and sets principles for the specific way accounting measures how individuals meet their responsibilities. Responsibility, however, is a wider and more personal moral matter of the individual (Lindkvist & Llewellyn, 2003). Consequently, acting accountable and acting responsible do not lead to the same actions, and both can be in place and have effects even when accounting information does not represent an economic truth, or even the economic performance of managers or the subunit.

Therefore, responsibility accounting mobilizes certain versions of what it means to act responsibly. This relates to which accounts the accountor gives and is expected to give and which accounts the accountor receives and expects to receive. But, as we see later in the book, acting responsibly means to act in an assemblage with many different, and often contradictory, possible directions. This problematizes accountability technologies, such as responsibility accounting, as means for making employees act responsibly. By using technologies that presume that accounting is the act of constructing representations, people who are made accountable by these means end up becoming instrumentally accountable and not acting as responsible managers. Organizations must therefore be careful with using accountability technologies and, instead, make employees accountable through reflective management practices instead of more systems-inspired approaches of developing instrumental and formalized accountability.

Accountability and responsibility

Accounting is a technology for constructing accountability relationships between managers and owners. "Accounting is a system designed to facilitate the smooth functioning of accountability relationships among interested parties" (Ijiri, 1975, p. ix).

Merchant and Otley (2007) describe similar accountability-orientation control systems and argue that control systems make people accountable for "their actions or for the results they or their organization produce" (p. 791).

Accountability is defined as the "liability to account for and answer for one's conduct, performance of duties, etc. (in modern use often with regard to parliamentary, corporate, or financial liability to the public, shareholders, etc.)" (*Oxford English Dictionary*, 2011a). Accountability, in this definition, related to broader concerns than the process of measuring and evaluating performance; it can be conceptualized more broadly than in terms of the effects of one's conduct on financial calculations. Toms (2014, p. 2) writes that

> accounting and accountability are ... the extension of the utilitarian "panopticon," assisting the task of social surveillance and

therefore the exercise of power, while accounting transitions are unintended outcomes produced by the strategic actions of a number of different participants.

In this way, accounting is understood as a means by which accountability relationships can be constructed, but at the same time it can be understood as a consequence of legitimizing social surveillance in society.

Accountability is arguably about giving accounts, and according to Munro (1996), this is something organizational members do hundreds of times a day in conversations and the exchange of opinions. In that way, making and giving accounts about who we are and what we are doing is a condition for participating in the social world (Wilmot, 1996), and, due to this, accountability is a widespread social practice. But accountability is also produced and evaluated through various calculations that allow for the constitution of what it means to *be* accountable – accountable in terms of what? Accounting is, in this sense, the calculation of targets that create "lines of 'visibility' into which participants are drawn by being held accountable ... for meeting these targets" (Munro, 1996, p. 3).

Accountability is an instrumental act of giving and receiving accounts of how well results are achieved. But responsibility is a wider concern connected to the moral dimension of acting in accordance with a set of values (Lindkvist & Llewellyn, 2003). These differences can also be found in the etymology of the words; accountability comes from accountable, which is a combination of *account* and *-able*. Accountable means to possess the capability of being subjected to perform the action of giving accounts. Most typically, accounts refer to a person's execution of their powers and duties (*Oxford English Dictionary*, 2011a, 2011b). Responsibility, on the other hand, comes from *responsible* and *-able* and means to be capable of fulfilling an obligation or duty. It is associated with carrying out actions in a 'morally principled or ethical way' (*Oxford English Dictionary*, 2010). Therefore, where accountability is associated with the act of giving and receiving accounts of one's conduct, responsibility is a matter of fulfilling one's obligation morally or ethically. Consequently, acting responsibly has connotations of moral and ethical actions, where accountability is more associated with the act and ability of giving accounts of one's actions.

The same points regarding responsibility are articulated in the philosophical literature. According to Derrida (1995), responsibility is not a simple thing. It can be thought of as a phenomenon between an individual and the other. He argues that there are no general principles that guide responsibility. His view challenges Lindkvist and Llewellyn's (2003) description of responsibility by arguing that values and ethically principled actions are also constructs, just as accounts of one's conduct are. Therefore, the point that accountability is more instrumental than responsibility is difficult to claim because, in the same way as accountability, values are also mediated.

Derrida (1995) argues that responsibility is singularity and responsibility is exposed to the problem of particularity versus universality; on the one hand, individuals can think of responsibility as a general kind of acting before 'the other' emerges, but as soon as a relation to 'the other' emerges, a paradox arises between universal responsibility and particular responsibility in the relation to 'the other'. This implies, for accountability and responsibility, that the distinction between the two is not possible to separate, but there is a tension between general, ethically principled responsibility based on values and acting responsibly according to different stakeholders. So, for Derrida (1995), acting responsibly is not a simple matter. It is not just a matter of acting in terms of one's duties, because the singularity of responsibility is both a general ethical concern and a particular concern emerging from relations with 'the other'.

In spite of this discussion, we consider accountability as the act of constructing, giving and receiving accounts of how well individuals meet the responsibility they are assigned. This relates to the particularity of responsibility. Thus, accountability is concerned with the justification of actions related to the responsibility individuals are assigned, whereas responsibility, even though it is a social construct, is a wider, and more personal, moral matter of the individual (Lindkvist & Llewellyn, 2003). The reason for making these conceptual distinctions between accountability and responsibility in relation to accounting is that accountability is linked to calculative practices that are simplifications of complex social relations (see, e.g., Kirk & Mouritsen, 1996; Quattrone, 2004). This means that responsibility in accounting is mediated by the transformation of interactions into, most often, numbers.

Research on the effects of performance measurement systems is sometimes divided into two theoretical streams: the ostensive research (accounting in principle) and the performative research (accounting in practice) (Catasús, 2008; Hansen, 2011). These two overall research streams are explained, with a particular focus on their different conceptualizations of how accountability is perceived within these streams, in the next sections.

The ostensive view on accountability

Ostensive theory builds on a presumption that "in principle, it is possible to discover properties which are typical of life in society, and could explain the social link and its evolution" (Hansen, 2011, p. 115).

This means that ostensive research applies a positivist understanding of reality as something "out there", and that theory consists of explanation and/or representations of that reality. Responsibility accounting is a theory that has emerged from ostensive theory. Responsibility accounting prescribes how responsibility center managers should be held accountable by means of performance measurement, which means that the performance of responsibility centers should be measured through specific calculations.

Responsibility accounting is about decentralizing decision rights to the departments and people in the organization, who have the most appropriate knowledge to make the best decisions. When allocating decision rights to a responsibility center manager, the information that is located in the decentralized parts of the organization is utilized by moving the decision rights to decentralized employees (Jensen & Meckling, 1995; Melumad, Mookherjee, & Reichelstein, 1992). The theory, therefore, suggests that a responsibility center design should be selected on the basis of the decision authority and specific knowledge in the different units of the organization. In order to be accountable for the decision rights assigned, there must be a close link between the decision rights assigned to the unit and the financial accounts used to assess the financial accountability of the business unit manager. Thus, the decision rights a business unit is assigned should be reflected in the broader financial responsibility of the business unit (Anthony & Govindarajan, 2003; Merchant & Van der Stede, 2007; Zimmerman, 2011). Therefore, responsibility accounting conceptualizes different responsibility centers, based on their decision authority. These amount to revenue and cost centers, profit centers and investment centers (Melumad et al., 1992).

Revenue centers have the responsibility of outputs without the ability to control inputs, whereas cost centers have the responsibility of inputs but without the ability to control outputs (sales) (Anthony & Govindarajan, 2003; Melumad et al., 1992). As the name indicates, revenue centers are measured on the revenue line of the profit and loss statement, which means that they are measured on their abilities to sell the product mix the company offers in the current market and find new markets for their products. But a revenue center is not responsible for the costs of the goods they sell.

Cost centers are measured in terms of their efficiency and effectiveness of processing inputs to products or services, but not selling them. Such centers include production departments as well as marketing departments, accounting departments, human resource departments and so on; therefore, cost centers must utilize the inputs to the extent the company finds appropriate (by setting standards or targets).

Through the use of responsibility accounting, a cost center's behavior is directed toward keeping up with these standards (Bulloch, 2006).

Profit centers are measured on profits, which means that the center's manager is accountable for both the revenue side and the cost side of the business unit (Jensen & Meckling, 1995; Melumad et al., 1992), as the profit measure is calculated as revenue minus costs. Therefore, profit centers typically have decision rights over both the cost side and the revenue side of the business unit. Revenue centers and cost centers can be changed to profit centers by using internal transfer prices in the internal transactions between different business units (Baker, Gibbons, & Murphy, 2001).

Responsibility accounting theory articulates the overarching principle that when a responsibility center is designed in a certain way, the behavior and decisions will align with the design and create desired behavioral effects. Therefore, an appropriate design of responsibility accounting will align decisions and job performance with the overall objectives of the organization (Merchant, 2006). The responsibility center design is considered significant in terms of framing the decision space of responsibility center managers.

The performative view on accountability

Performative theory builds on relational ontology (Hansen, 2011) from, for example, actor-network theory. The point here is that the performance of something, such as performance indicators, is constituted not by its inherent composition but by the relations it renders to other actors within and outside the organization (Chua, 1995; Quattrone & Hopper, 2006; Robson, 1991, 1992).

Kirk and Mouritsen (1996) study performance measurement as a technology used to construct accountable managers. They show how accountability is orchestrated within accounting information, but also outside it, because not everything can be counted within the calculations, and in that sense the accountable manager becomes accountable for much more than what is inscribed in the performance calculations. The calculation is a generalization of the complexity the manager acts within, and the manager must act both with a concern for the effects of the actions on his or her performance indicators (which is a 'regime of truth' that shapes what decisions count) but also on the idiosyncratic knowledge of the local conditions of their market.

Messner (2009) argues that "the reasons why somebody has taken a particular course of action are not entirely clear to this person herself" and stresses that this creates an ethical problem associated with the widespread idea that more accountability is good. Messner resonates with Derrida in describing the relation between knowledge and decisions, and argues that the need for (managers') decisions emerges when the calculative logic ends, or when it is incomplete. In that respect, the decision itself is crucial only in situations where the decision cannot be derived from knowledge. As Messner (2009, p. 925) says, "it may be based on knowledge (and often should), but at one point, there will be the need to go beyond this knowledge and to take the risk of making a decision". Thus, there would be no need for decisions if knowledge about the decision were entirely adequate. Therefore, it is because of the inadequacy of knowledge that a person is needed to make the decision.

Being responsible for many more circumstances than the economic calculations count contains a paradox. Although accounting calculations constitute a basis for categorizing actions and results as good or bad at the general level, managers must still act on the particular movements they see in their environment, which may or may not be justified on the basis of economic calculations that do not take into account these movements because the calculations are estimations and aggregations and therefore generalizations that do not count faithfully the particularities of practice (c.f. Deleuze, 2004; Messner, 2009). We see some implications of this in the work of Quattrone and Hopper (2006), who show how the heterogeneity of practice is continuously challenging management accounting practice and generates performances we cannot anticipate. Therefore, the creation of more or less stable accountability inscriptions is problematic, because practice is always drifting in various directions (which is elaborated in the work of Andon, Baxter and Chua (2007)).

Actor-network theory is not the only inspiration for performative accounting research. Foucault's scholarship is also influential, for example, in the works of Miller and O'Leary (1987), Miller and O'Leary (1994) and Miller (2001). While actor-network theory and this chapter are concerned predominantly with the fluidity and emergence of phenomena and performances, the Foucauldian literature is mainly concerned with how things become discursive (Miller & O'Leary, 1987). Even though there seems to be a distinct difference between Foucault's scholarship and this book's approach, some parts of Foucault's writings are closely related to Deleuze's line of reasoning (e.g., Deleuze, 2004; Deleuze & Guattarí, 2004). This is demonstrated by Mennicken and Miller (2012) who touch upon the territorializing performance of accounting. Predominantly, Foucault's writings are about discourse as stabilization in epochs, which also resonates with Miller and O'Leary's (1994) notion of temporary stability of assemblages. Deleuze's point of departure is fluidity and emerging characteristics, performance and organizing of things and phenomena. In this sense, this chapter elaborates and extends the discussions on the performativity (consequences/effects) of performance measurement systems, with attention on how responsibility accounting's ideals of responsibility center designs and effects are challenged by the particular circumstances of the practice in which they are mobilized. This is done by analyzing the case study from the point of view of assemblage theory, drawing on DeLanda's (2006) development of Deleuze's scholarship to theorize on social phenomena.

References

Andon, P., Baxter, J., & Chua, W. F. (2007). Accounting change as relational drift: A field study of experiments with performance measurement. *Management Accounting Research, 18*(2), 273–308.

Anthony, R., & Govindarajan, V. (2003). *Management Control Systems* (11th ed.). New York, NY: McGraw-Hill.

Baker, G., Gibbons, R., & Murphy, K. J. (2001). Bringing the market inside the firm? *American Economic Review, 91*(2), 212–218.

Bulloch, J. (2006). Responsibility accounting – A results-oriented appraisal system. *Human Resource Management, 2*(4), 25–31.

Catasús, B. (2008). In search of accounting absence. *Critical Perspectives on Accounting, 19*(7), 1004–1019.

Chang, L.-c. (2007). The NHS performance assessment framework as a balanced scorecard approach: Limitations and implications. *International Journal of Public Sector Management, 20*(2), 101–117.

Chua, W. (1995). Experts, networks and inscriptions in the fabrication of accounting images: A story of the representation of three public hospitals. *Accounting, Organizations and Society, 20*(2–3), 111–145.

Deleuze, G. (2004). *Difference and Repetition*. New York, NY: Continuum.

Deleuze, G., & Guattarí, F. (2004). *A Thousand Plateaus*. New York, NY: Continuum.

Derrida, J. (1995). *The Gift of Death*. Chicago: University of Chicago Press.

Hansen, A. (2011). Relating performative and ostensive management accounting research: Reflections on case study methodology. *Qualitative Research in Accounting & Management, 8*(2), 108–138.

Ijiri, Y. (1975). *Theory of Accounting Measurement*. Sarasota: American Accounting Association.

Jensen, M. C., & Meckling, W. H. (1995). Specific and general knowledge, and organizational structure. *Journal of Applied Corporate Finance, 8*(2), 4–18.

Kirk, K., & Mouritsen, J. (1996). Spaces of Accountability: Accounting Systems and Systems of Accountability in a Multinational. In R. Munro & J. Mouritsen (Eds.), *Accountability. Power, Ethos and Technologies of Managing* (201–224). London: International Thomson Business Press.

Lindkvist, L., & Llewellyn, S. (2003). Accountability, responsibility and organization. *Scandinavian Journal of Management, 19*(2), 251–273.

Melumad, N., Mookherjee, D., & Reichelstein, S. (1992). A theory of responsibility centers. *Journal of Accounting and Economics, 15*(4), 445–484.

Mennicken, A., & Miller, P. (2012). Accounting, territorialization and power. *Foucault Studies, 13*, 4–24.

Merchant, K. A. (2006). Measuring general managers' performances: Market, accounting and combination-of-measures systems. *Accounting, Auditing & Accountability Journal, 19*(6), 893–917.

Merchant, K. A., & Otley, D. T. (2007). A Review of the Literature on Control and Accountability. In C. S. Chapman, A. G. Hopwood & M. D. Shields (Eds.), *Handbook of Management Accounting Research*. Oxford, UK: Elsevier, 785–802.

Merchant, K. A., & Van der Stede, W. A. (2007). *Management Control Systems*. Harlow, England: Prentice Hall.

Messner, M. (2009). The limits of accountability. *Accounting, Organizations and Society, 34*(8), 918–938.

Miller, P., & O'Leary, T. (1994). The factory as laboratory. *Science in Context, 7*(3), 469–496.

Miller, P. B. (2001). Governing by numbers: Why calculative practices matter. *Social Research, 68*(2), 379–396.

Miller, P. B., & O'Leary, T. (1987). Accounting and the construction of the governable person. *Accounting, Organizations and Society, 12*(3), 235–265.

Munro, R. (1996). Alignment and identity work: The study of accounts and accountability. In R. Munro & J. Mouritsen (Eds.), *Accountability. Power, Ethos and Technologies of Managing* (1–19). London: International Thomson Business Press.

Oxford English Dictionary: Accountability, n. (2011a). Online (www.oed.com).

Oxford English Dictionary: Accountable, adj. (2011b). Online (www.oed.com).

Oxford English Dictionary: Responsible, adj. and n. (2010). Online (www.oed.com).

Quattrone, P. (2004). Accounting for God: accounting and accountability practices in the Society of Jesus (Italy, XVI–XVII centuries). *Accounting, Organizations and Society, 29*(7), 647–683.

Quattrone, P., & Hopper, T. (2006). What is IT? SAP, accounting, and visibility in a multinational organisation. *Information and Organization, 16*(3), 212–250.

Roberts, J. (2009). No one is perfect: The limits of transparency and an ethic for 'intelligent' accountability. *Accounting, Organizations and Society, 34*(8), 957–970.

Robson, K. (1991). On the arenas of accounting change: The process of translation. *Accounting, Organizations and Society, 16*(5–6), 547–570.

Robson, K. (1992). Accounting numbers as 'inscription': Action at a distance and the development of accounting. *Accounting, Organizations and Society, 17*(7), 685–708.

Toms, S. (2014). Accounting and Capitalism. In C. L. Cooper (Ed.), *Wiley Encyclopedia of Management* (1). John Wiley and Sons (Wiley Online Library, https://onlinelibrary.wiley.com/doi/10.1002/9781118785317.weom010066).

Willmott, H. (1996). Thinking accountability: Accounting for the disciplined production of self. In Munro, R., Mouritsen, J. (Eds.), *Accountability: Power, Ethos and Technologies of Managing* (23–39). London: International Thompson Publishing.

Zimmerman, J. L. (2011). *Accounting for Decision Making and Control* (7th ed.). New York, NY: McGraw-Hill.

Part II
Empirical plateaus

5 Territorializing accountability[1]

This chapter and Chapter 6 are based on data from a one-and-a-half-year ethnographic case study of the responsibility center and its organizational significance in a Danish company. Throughout participant observation along with a series of interviews with managers, I placed attention on how managers take responsibility for making decisions and the space of possibilities[2] regarding the decisions. In developing the empirical storyline, I am inspired by science and technology studies, where the Deleuzian scholarship is capable of providing important contributions. Williams (2003) problematizes the boundaries of knowledge by "folding the limit back on to the core of knowledge and on to our settled understanding of the true and the good". I aim to do this by performing what Deleuze calls "folding texts onto each other" (Deleuze & Guattarí, 2004, p. 6); by doing so, I aim to explore how controversies – in relation to regimes of signs and territorializations – occur. To be more specific, assemblage theory is mobilized to organize the case study. This provides a way to discuss how assemblages of accountability are constructed by different entities and how the entities within the assemblage are signified (e.g., what calculations mean), and how the assemblage of accountability creates territorializations that affect managers' decision space. The chapter ends with a discussion of how responsibility accounting is brought into effect not only by its design but also by the interventions in the accountability assemblage, which affect and transform how managers experience what it means to be 'accountable', and for what one is accountable.

The case company

To ensure anonymity, I use the pseudonym Disability Corp. Denmark to refer to the case company. This company is a subsidiary of an international group, Disability Corp. International, who is owned by

Disability Tech. Holding. Disability Corp. International and Disability Tech. Holding both have headquarters in another European Union (EU) country. The group has several production subsidiaries that produce high-tech equipment for disabled people; all of these production facilities are located in Asia. Like the Danish sales subsidiary, Disability Corp. has individual subsidiaries in all European countries. Due to this structure, Disability Corp. Denmark is responsible for sales in the Danish market.

Internally, the Danish subsidiary is organized as a profit center and they are allocated the decision rights to control all line items in their budget. Back in 2009, they had very high autonomy in decision-making. This meant they could spend money on whatever they found necessary in order to reach the level of profit that the headquarters had approved in the budgeting process. During the case study, the company had an average full-time equivalent (FTE) count of 52, where 9 were managers, each with a responsibility for product lines or departments such as administration, accounting and service.

The products the company produces and sells on the Danish market are high-tech equipment for disabled people. In the Danish market, this equipment is paid for by the public sector, either the full cost or a partial payment. An end user can choose to get the equipment either from a public hospital or from a private hospital. Private hospitals typically have shorter waiting lists for treatment, and, therefore, end users will get the equipment faster than through public hospitals. In private hospitals, end users pay a part of the cost of the equipment themselves and the rest is paid through reimbursement from the public sector that goes directly to the private hospital. The reimbursement price is a fixed amount, independent of which technological class the product belongs to. This means that if end users get the equipment from the private hospital, the reimbursement covers approximately the cost of the cheapest variant of the product. If the end user wants an item from a better product category (in terms of quality or technology), they must pay the cost difference between the cheapest and the more expensive variant themselves.

The storyline of how managerial responsibility unfolds in Disability Corp. Denmark is described in the rest of this chapter. This is structured around aspects in the organization that constitute 'becoming accountable' in the company, which highlights the territorialization process of what it means to be an accountable manager in the subsidiary. The chapter focuses on the process of 'becoming accountable' to underline the Deleuzian point that 'accountability' of managers is potentially always changing and transforming to something new, which I investigate through the empirical material. The storyline is therefore structured according to the episodes that had significance for managerial responsibility in the responsibility center. The focus here is on how the significance of accountability in the responsibility accounting organization continuously changes when the distribution of managerial responsibility is put into practice.

There are circumstances related to both planning the budget and evaluating employee performance, and intervening in decision-making, which all together had an impact on what 'becoming account-able' means, and also impacted the responsibilities that managers were considered to be accountable for.

Becoming accountable through delegating and evaluating budget responsibility

Planning the budget change

The Danish subsidiary was not using budgets as a tool for performance evaluation of managers before the case study began. Accountability as formalized in accounting structures had been totally absent and, hence, deterritorialized. The former Chief Executive Officer (CEO) and Chief Financial Officer (CFO) decided not to do this in a formalized way and had a very laissez-faire management style. They kept the budget responsibility at their own desks without delegating it further down to the sales managers. Managers had been expected to perform their jobs satisfactorily without the delegation of budget responsibility, and this had been a successful management style until this point. The administration and HR manager explained how the laissez-faire management style had survived and how the responsibility structure could not be assembled in a more formalized manner because the general ledger table was very messy and this had made it impossible for the CFO and CEO to delegate budget responsibility:

HR MANAGER: Actually, I am responsible for the administration and what we use there. But because it has been so badly set up in the system (the Accounting information system), I have never had a budget to work after. So that is really difficult. No one can even tell me on the different items, what we used last year on the different items. Because all of it lies in one big messy heap.

(Interview, January 2010, parentheses added)

Thus, formalized responsibility inscribed in the accounting system was deterritorialized because of the messy account numbers. While budget responsibility was not delegated to the managers, they still believed they knew what was expected of them:

NJL: But even though they didn't have a budget they still knew what was expected of them as sales managers?

HR MANAGER: Yes, what they should sell. They knew that of course. They also knew what their sales numbers were. But they didn't know what they spent their money on.

(Interview, January 2010)

However, some efforts were made in assembling accountability in a more formalized way. There has been a certain amount of planning of marketing and sales expenditures, even though managers at that time did not have any responsibility for spending levels:

NJL: How do you manage as manager? I could hear you have some sales numbers you have to meet or which you have set as targets. How do you follow up on that?

SALES MANAGER: Do you mean activities, campaigns etc.?

NJL: Yes but also for example if you have some KPI's or performance measures or something besides what you have talked about already. And budget etc.

SALES MANAGER: What we do with these performance measures, if we should just call them that. Year after year we plan activities, which is going to happen the single year. And that depends a little bit of how the market development is. We look after that when we are in the field. Especially in the production industry. And when we feel like having a grasp of how the pulse of the market is, then we plan our marketing strategy after that. Marketing and sales strategy. And then, once every year, we write down how our activities look, what the target group and purpose with the activity is ad what the expected output is on the things. That is essentially the management tool they have on overall basis in relation to what we are going to do when and at what point of time. And then we delegate the tasks internally in the team: who can, relative to other customers etc. etc., participate in those activities.

(Interview, January 2010)

The manager responsible for store and logistics supported the point that the management has been laissez-faire. He explained how the store workers recorded invoices in the books:

STORE MANAGER: They get the article scanned and makes the invoice balance and those things and then they record it ... We'll get them recorded, if it is going to be stocked or not.

NJL: ok. Is there a budget for that?

STORE MANAGER: Yes there is, probably, somewhere. It is not something.

NJL: Not something you are engaged with?

STORE MANAGER: No, no.

(Interview, January 2010)

While this interview passage is about who did the registration of invoices, it shows quite clearly that the store manager did not get much information about budget capacities or constraints related to his areas of responsibility. He managed the stock and logistics without considering budget implications, at least not directly. Again, this signifies that accountability was assembled in a manner where the manager's primary responsibility was to make sure the stock orders were recorded and make sure the logistics functioned well, without considering the impacts of this on the profit-loss statement or how these effects could be improved. His managerial responsibility was therefore assembled in a way where he was concerned with the quality of the activities he managed. It was not translated into an accountability relationship based on financial numbers.

The store manager later explained that his main focus on stock and logistics was to minimize decentralized stock because "it is better that the articles get to the place where they have an overview of where the group can sell them at the moment". This means that the Danish manager would not order more than the absolute minimum they needed. To make this stock management concern possible (which in Deleuzian terms is how this concern was territorialized in the practical setting) without having customers waiting too long on their products (which could be a potential source of deterritorialization of this managerial concern), they needed to have several different delivery methods: 'China', 'Vietnam', 'truck' and 're-truck'. Truck is used when they need articles but cannot wait for delivery from Asia (they come instead from a central stock room in Europe) and re-truck is for articles needed, which did not come with the first truck order (also from the central stock room in Europe). Their use of "truck" and "re-truck" to coordinate centralized and decentralized stock shows that the practice was built on the premise of territorializing the managerial concern of minimizing local stock, but that doing so required flexibility in delivery methods.

But this also led to an internal financial question in Disability Corp. Denmark, namely whether it would be cheaper to build more local stock versus the costs of frequent truck deliveries (Disability Corp. Denmark was charged for the transportation costs). Neither the CFO nor the logistics manager could answer this question, because the accounting system could not provide data that could help them resolve this. The point here is threefold. First, it shows that territorializing a managerial concern needs to align the practice with the concern (which is immaterial), but second, it also shows that the decision space, which could potentially reterritorialize the practice given that the management team could create credible arguments, is constrained by the possibility of making things calculable. Third, it shows that even though the decision in this setting is financial, is it not tied to budget concerns. Thus, financial accountability is present in a non-formalized way, even in these situations where accounting is absent.

One last matter to consider before explaining in more detail how the responsibility assemblage was changed is the notion of the 'laissez-faire' management. Identifying the management style as 'laissez-faire' could be read as an undesirable or inadequate way of rendering managers accountable for their managerial actions. But this is not the point. Rather, the 'laissez-faire' approach shows how an 'accountable manager' can take on different significations depending on the assemblage it unfolds within. In the laissez-faire assemblage in Disability Corp. Denmark, certain things were obligatory, such as keeping a certain stock and satisfying customers, while other things were optional, such as keeping track of the financial effects within the limits of the budget. Thus, the responsibility of managing store and logistics was not about being a cost center and sticking within a certain cost budget, but about making sure the subsidiary could continue to deliver high service to customers in terms of security of supply. Thus, managerial attention focused on how well the departments conducted their core activities.

Changing the budget structure

In 2009 the CFO in Disability Corp. Denmark together with the CEO decided to change the means by which managers were made responsible. They did so because they had faced high growth over the past ten years and had become a large organization. Moreover, they had developed a new strategy plan through which they expected higher growth rates. Based on the historical growth and future expectations, they chose to change the responsibility structure to provide the management team with more detailed financial information about their departments' performance relative to the budget under these new conditions. Thus, what happened was the very beginning of a deter-ritorialization of how accountability had previously been actualized.

They planned to introduce a new budgeting practice where the country's budget would be delegated to managers and followed up on a monthly basis. As mentioned, the Danish subsidiary was managed as a profit center, and, according to the CFO, the purpose of the new budgeting practice was to delegate the responsibility for meeting the subsidiary's budget targets to the departments responsible for selling the different product categories. The department managers should have a proportion of the overall budget allocated to them and be re-sponsible for achieving the goals set in the budget process. They im-plemented this new responsibility structure in the winter of 2009/2010, and their plan was to start it formally in the budget year 2010/2011, which started April 1, 2010.

Almost all managers accepted the new responsibility structure the budget outlined. The reason for that, according to the CFO, was that virtually all managers were new in their positions and had not been accustomed to the former management style. The only manager who had prior experience as manager in Disability Corp. Denmark had actually expressed opposition to the new budget practice. But he had been pressed by the Danish top management to adapt to the new man-agement practice.

The budget for 2010/2011 was prepared by the Danish management team and afterward reviewed and adapted by Disability Internation-al's accounting department with the Danish managers' accepting the changes.

Thus, it seemed that the new accountability structure would be as-sembled in a reasonable way in terms of making managers financially accountable, which had been the initial purpose of making these for-mal control changes – in Latourian terms to make action at a distance possible (Robson, 1992). But as time went on, the managers' budget numbers became a larger and larger problem for them:

CFO: If we look at our allocation, no not allocation, the division of the budget in the individual areas, it is a bit more problematic that we had thought.

NJL: How?

CFO: When we prepared the budget last year in December/January the manager team we have now, they were all of them here, but some of them were new. And it was not taken very serious and it has been hard to get some plans to add up with what they think now, half a year later and after they have acquainted themselves with the business compared with when we (prepared the numbers) departed from what we have done in the past, because that was what we used as a basis for the numbers. Therefore the reality has become a little bit distanced from what we thought. You know, a little bit too distanced. The tendency is that they think new thoughts every 2nd month. Especially the marketing and sales budget is problematic.

NJL: What about sales?

CFO: Sales are allocated ok and we know who is responsible for which sale and the goals for each month are meaningful. They are too high ... but that's how it is.

(Interview, September 2010)

Following this excerpt, the CFO argued that the market had moved to become even more privatized than it had been in the preceding year. This movement affected the types of products (e.g., the technological features) that their customers demanded. The products people buy from private clinics were generally from a cheaper product category, and therefore, their sales targets in terms of turnover turned out to be too high. This became important for the assemblage of managerial responsibility partly due to the reason that this affected the revenue, but also due to the effects this had on the profitability, because of the internal transfer pricing rules, which we will see later.

Evaluating performance

Before the budgeting period started, the budget was inscribed on certain conditions about the market. The market assembled in a different form than the budget inscriptions envisaged, for example, in relation to the proportion of the market that was privatized and the market prices of the products. As one of the managers explained, the group's accounting department intervened with the subsidiary and placed certain obligations on the managers about which activities to conduct in order to try to resolve the problem with variances between budgets and actual performance:

CFO: As long as we have reasonable results the group's accounting department stays away from details but sets some lines of direction.

NJL: Control wise they are open as long as you are performing well?

CFO: As long as it is going ok they have kept themselves away.

(Interview, June 2010)

The Danish CFO explained that the problem did not seem to be because of managers' shirking or because managers were considered to be making 'bad' managerial decisions (as the group's accounting department's interventions could indicate), but rather, in theoretical terms, because the model and the world were moving in different directions. While the managers should act upon these directions, the group's accounting department did not possess any knowledge about them, as they did not know the Danish market conditions (which were radically different from other European countries). This is discussed later in relation to the marketing budget.

In the financial year 2011/2012, where the new responsibility structure was set, the budgets were specified as line-item budgets, grouped by departments. The Danish subsidiary was still formally managed as a profit center. But being a 'responsible manager' changed in the responsibility center, as an effect of the movements happening in different aspects of the accountability assemblage. In the evaluation of the 2011/2012 budget, it was clear that department managers were responsible for much more than financial profits; the budget Key Performance Indicators (KPIs) specified budget targets for each line in the income statement and calculated budgeted gross profit II, gross profit margin and earnings before interest, taxes and amortization (EBITA). This meant that the managers became accountable for every single line in the budget and were evaluated on the performance of every single line, even though their objective was to make profit and thus concentrate on the profit line.

Interrupting financial accountability: transfer prices

Yet another important matter related to the assemblage of 'being a responsible manager' is the lever of managing profit through the means of pricing. The implications of the calculation of prices and product costs problematize the ideal of accounting calculations as 'representations' of financial issues related to the activities that happen between the company and customers (in Chapter 3 accounting as representation or re-presentation was discussed).

In Disability Corp. Denmark, the calculation of profit became another hindrance for the stabilization of the accountability assemblage, due to issues in their process of calculating transfer prices. The transfer pricing issue was specifically related to the prices the Danish subsidiary bought the products it sold at from the production subsidiaries. Nobody, including the Danish CFO, believed the transfer pricing calculation resulted in 'true' manufacturing costs and thus 'true' profit estimates. This became an obstacle in the provision of information to decision-making. To explore this point, I started by looking at how profitability in terms of revenues and costs developed and how managers considered these accounting elements.

The budget process ended with headquarters (HQ) approving the yearly budget for the Danish subsidiary in February each year. After the approval, HQ's accountants began their work to optimize the transfer prices with the aim of reducing tax payments in Denmark (the corporation tax is lower in Germany), of course while staying within the legal boundaries of International Financial Reporting Standards (IFRS) (Interview, April 2010). The CFO indicated that this transfer pricing practice induced a problem for the managers:

NJL: How are the budgets specified? Do they have some overall sales targets to meet and do they have some costs they...

CFO: They can spend, yes.

NJL: Is it only marketing costs?

CFO: No it is all the costs they, more or less, have an influence on. Of course there is a grey zone and we are not precisely aware of what is in the grey zone but there are salaries, there are marketing costs, there are travel expenses, there are telephone costs, cars for their sales staff, yes, entertainment costs. You know, unit variable costs are not included in this exercise because it is determined not so much of, you know, if you sell one or another product within the product line does not mean very much because it is a transfer price setting according to the model that says it has to result in the right bottom line. And we get the same contribution margin in percentage terms independent on which product they sell.

(Interview, April 2010)

In this quote, a question was raised regarding the relationship between transfer prices and how the cost represents what it 'purports to represent'. Later, this became a larger problem for profit calculations than the CFO explained in this interview. The CFO did not believe the transfer price to be a reliable component in the description of profit. In an interview, he explained that the contribution margin that came out of the transfer price calculation was essentially the same for each product:

NJL: The sales departments are only oriented towards sales prices. They are not charged for the purchase prices, I mean, the prices you pay internally to the production subsidiaries for the products?

CFO: No. We have a transfer price model where the margin in percent is the same on every product. But, of course it is better to sell
more high-tech products than low-tech in terms of money, but if
we count so much on money as we do then if they sell for 100.000
DKK, if it is one or another product they sold is irrelevant for how
much we get in contribution ratio.

(Interview, September 2010)

Internally, in the Danish subsidiary, the CFO calculated contribution
margins on products by deducting the transfer price from the sales
price. But the transfer price was set to minimize tax payments in
Denmark, and, therefore, the contribution margin ended up being a
product of the transfer price calculation rather than an accurate representation of the contribution margin of the company's products.
This made the CFO believe the contribution margins and, as a consequence, the annual results were wrong, which was a problem for decisions related to exploiting price changes to gain more profit:

NJL: If you change the price with 10 percent would the transfer price
then be changed 10 percent too?
CFO: Yes, but only once a year. That is important. Because if you start
to change it continually the tax hammer will fall.
NJL: Yes. It is a bit complicated with the transfer prices.
CFO: It is very complicated. The problem is, then the managers come
and ask me, 'look, I am buying this product at that price from
Germany. That means I have a lot of space to offer discounts and
still earn money on it' eh, yes ... eh.
NJL: Yes that's a bit hard to answer.
CFO: That's a bit hard, or 'should I rather sell'...
NJL: Don't you know the real costs?
CFO: I don't know the real costs so that they can come and ask 'which
of those two should I sell?' (Gesticulates that he cannot answer).
NJL: That's interesting.
CFO: Yes, that's very, that's a bit awkward.

(Interview, September 2010)

As the interview quote indicates, the company's transfer pricing practice meant that the CFO literally did not know the prices at which
products would give a positive contribution to the group. Therefore, he
could not guide the lower level managers about which product prices
to offer. This was a concern that deterritorialized the possibilities of
acting financially responsible in managerial decisions.

To address this issue, the CFO decided to allocate all product costs to the budget that he himself was responsible for. As the CFO argued, the implication of the transfer price calculation was that managers could not control the contribution margin of their products and should therefore not be held accountable for it. But this was surprising because Disability Corp. Denmark was managed as a profit center, and their main concern should therefore be to generate profit, not revenue only. But because profit was calculated as their contribution margin minus operating expenses, the responsibility that was articulated through the financial numbers became messy, and the CFO did not believe that the contribution margin was a 'true' representation of the economic situation of the group.

A practical implication of their method of calculating transfer prices with the 'same' contribution margin ratio on each product was related to situations with decreasing sales; if they reduced their prices to increase their sales, but did not sell more units than planned, or if their sales moved from a more expensive product group to a less expensive product group, the net income would decrease and even become negative. This was not necessarily because the financial impact on the group would reflect this, but because the transfer prices were fixed and changed only once per year. Therefore, the CFO did not feel that the profit calculations were very helpful to inform better managerial decisions, especially in situations where competitors pushed their prices down.

Market opportunities and the profit calculation

The CFO raised a point about the complexity of the profitability calculation and its ability to distinguish market opportunities with positive financial effects from negative financial effects (i.e., where to sell products, how many to sell and at what price). The point in this incident in Disability Corp. is that profit opportunity exists in the market, but these opportunities should be exploited by the managers only to the extent that they contribute positively to the group's overall result.

The problem for the CFO was that the profit calculation calculates profit as the difference between sales price and transfer price. Therefore, the company did not know when a reduction of prices would still contribute positively to the financial results in the group or which product mix would give the highest profit. Would it be more profitable to sell the cheaper, low-tech products or would it be more profitable to sell expensive, high-tech products? Due to the problems of not having a representative manufacturing cost to follow, the CFO's approach to the problem ended up being based on the accounting information he had available:

CFO: we get the same contribution margin in percentage terms independent on which product they sell. Of course it would be better if everything they sold was the most expensive product but we recognize that by rewarding them to an extent for selling up ... We use the term average selling price a lot. The higher the average selling price, the higher the profit. Because the selling price, no, our purchase price is set as a percentage of the selling price.

(Interview, April 2010)

The CFO explained that it would be better for the Danish subsidiary if managers sold more expensive products. But they did not know how the decision affected the profitability of the group, which was also an important concern for them. The consequence of this was a reduction of their decision freedom; when they thought a change of prices could be beneficial, they turned to HQ to get the price changes approved:

CFO: If we can feel we have to change the price significantly then we must take the discussion with Germany about whether they will allow us to reduce the price so much. To get in to that market and stay on the market or forget that market.

(Interview, September 2010)

To sum up this incident, the consequence of the transfer pricing practice was that the decision rights of price changes moved back to HQ, even though the Danish profit center should be able to control this themselves to exploit the market opportunities in the local market. Because of the transfer price, Disability Corp. Denmark was not able to make economic decisions related to profitability on other lines in the budget than the revenue line (operating expenses were not variable during the budget period). Altogether, this meant that managers ended up being accountable for a budget that they could hardly control. They controlled their own activities, but the levers the German accounting department used to make subsidiaries report to them and to minimize transfer prices made the market opportunities very difficult for the Danish managers to exploit, due to the complexity and messiness of the information available. Therefore, the financial responsibility became reterritorialized in the sense that the managers and the CFO in the subsidiary ended up being concerned with the revenue line only.

Notes

1 The empirical material in this chapter and Chapter 6 comes from a larger research project, which has been published in the *Scandinavian Journal of Management*. Some portions of the text, such as interview excerpts, have previously been published in "Lennon, N. J. (2019). Responsibility accounting, managerial action and 'a counter-ability': Relating the physical and virtual spaces of decision-making. *Scandinavian Journal of Management, 35* (3), 101062" (with permission from Elsevier).

2 Space of possibilities regarding decisions is the concept that concerns the decisions managers have the ability to take. *Space of possibilities* is elaborated by DeLanda (2006, p. 29). Here it means that the decision space, or space of possibilities, constitutes the decision possibilities managers can choose.

References

DeLanda, M. (2006). *A New Philosophy of Society*. New York, NY: Continuum International Publishing Group.

Deleuze, G., & Guattari, F. (2004). *A Thousand Plateaus*. New York, NY: Continuum.

Robson, K. (1992). Accounting numbers as "inscription": Action at a distance and the development of accounting. *Accounting, Organizations and Society, 17*(7), 685–708.

Williams, J. (2003). *Gilles Deleuze's difference and Repetition a Critical Introduction and Guide*. Edinburgh: Edinburgh University Press.

6 Deterritorializing accountability[1]

Accounting theory argues that designing accountability structures in a certain way, by making managers accountable for certain cost and revenue accounts, frames the decision space in a way that allows managers to control what they are held accountable for, and that this (controllability) is a reasonable design criterion for the management control system (Merchant, 2006). This principle also resonates in the responsibility center design where profit centers are held accountable for both costs and revenue, and the focus is therefore on generating profit. In revenue centers, the cost side is of less importance to the center manager(s), because the managers are held accountable for generating revenue only. Nonetheless, the freedom to act and make decisions with such an accounting regime is a fragile construct. In Disability Corp., we see that the decision space is influenced by different interventions from headquarters (HQ), which deterritorialize the decision space of the managers by changing the boundaries of what is allowed and what is decided by other people in the organization. This means that the decision authority of managers becomes a constant negotiation between the different stakeholders in the accountability assemblage. Thus, as I will describe below, different actions that relate to the accountability assemblage continually change the managers' decision freedom by displacing decision rights back and forth between HQ and the subsidiary and displacing them between managers within the Danish subsidiary.

The budget letter

As mentioned, the HQ of Disability Corp. decided to intervene with the decisions and actions in the Danish subsidiary when the monthly financial reports did not meet the targets set in the budgeting process. This was not the only intervention led by HQ into the subsidiary's budget. One very important object that potentially deterritorialized the managerial decision rights was the budget letter.

Every financial year, the first thing that happens in the budget process is that HQ sends a budget letter to the subsidiaries, in which they outline different activities that should be carried out during the next financial year. The activities outlined in the budget letter were required to be financed by money from the managers' marketing budgets. An example of how HQ intervened through the budget letter is visible in the budget letter for the financial year 2012/2013. The budget letter explains the group's expectations to the local subsidiaries' performance.

The introduction section of the letter argues that the growth in local currencies was good in the financial year 2011/2012, but because of some currency concerns relative to some currencies in the subsidiary's countries, the group's growth in profit and earnings before interest, tax and amortization (EBITA) had decreased significantly. Based on this problem, the budget letter states that the following year had to create substantially higher profitability levels. These were to be achieved through growth in the revenue line and cost management (Budget Letter 2012/2013).

The budget letter explains that the increase in operating expenditure (OPEX) in 2011/2012 came from sales force and customer service headcount increases, as well as investments in structures and processes to make the organization scalable. The cost increase exceeded the revenue increases, and, therefore, they stressed that the target profitability would increase in the following year.

Additionally, the budget letter states that subsidiaries are not allowed to budget with net increases in headcount. If increased headcount would be needed, a business case must be provided that "proves the additional headcount will boost your sales growth over the targeted growth rate" (Budget Letter 2012/2013). This is obviously important for managerial responsibility and accountability, as it is a move toward reducing the decision freedom in the profit center by stating explicit requirements to their cost structures, and therefore, it is another step toward deterritorializing the managerial decision space.

The budget letter also provided explicit requirements to the revenue targets for different product lines. The overall sales growth of the Disability Corp. International product line was expected to be set at eight to ten percent. In a supplement to the budget letter, which was specific for the Scandinavian countries, the target revenue growth was even higher; in Denmark it was set to 20 percent.[2]

Through these different requirements, the budget letter 2012/2013 transformed the practical unfolding of accountability. While accountability in Disability Corp. Denmark initially was about delegating responsibility to managers to act on local conditions, it transformed into a calculative act of delivering the financial performance planned in the budgeting process.

The right to money – spending the marketing budget

This episode happened simultaneously with the deterritorialization described above. Therefore, we take a step back to 2010/2011 here to describe circumstances related to the right to spend money and the relationship between this and the deterritorialization of the assemblage of managerial responsibility.

The CFO expressed problems related to the sales and marketing budget. As mentioned earlier, the majority of the managers were new in their positions when the budget 2010/2011 was planned, and therefore, many of them did not have any experience about which budget targets to use to 'represent' reasonable sales possibilities in the market. Nonetheless, the management team allocated the budgeted revenue and costs between them and got the budget approved by HQ with some adjustments where HQ found the development from the last financial year too low.

According to one of the Danish managers, HQ did not have specific knowledge about the Danish market, but the people there still intervened in the budgeting process by adjusting the draft that the CEO and CFO had brought with them to the 'budget week' at HQ. The point of adjusting the draft was to make sure the budget targets would result in the desired financial effects, such as gross profit, OPEX and cash flow (Interview with CFO, 2010). In this way, the adjustment and acceptance from HQ was not about considering the market opportunities but about making sure that budgets were composed so that they would set the directions to achieve desired financial results in terms of providing a satisfactory return on the investments made over the past years.

Initially, the CFO did not see the budget allocation or target setting as a problem. But at the meetings where the Danish managers got their marketing and sales budget allocated to their departments, they could not cope with the implications for their future sales performance. The territorialization of this new practice started to weaken. The CFO explained a problem related to this:

CFO: Let's start in the positive way. Regarding the monthly follow up we had the idea that we should use the format of sending sales numbers and expenditure numbers out and then the managers should comments on a front page (of the excel report) about what money they have used and why they have sold so much or not so much. And the format and templates work fine. If we look at the part regarding allocation, or not allocation, division of the budget between areas, it is a bit more problematic than we expected.

NJL: How?

CFO: We never got the original budget divided and an accept that it was going to be like that.

(Interview, September 2010)

The process of allocation of marketing budgets created two problems that pushed the deterritorialization further. The first problem occurred because the activities they had planned to be held in the 2010/2011 budget year were mainly decided on the basis of what they had done the year before, and from the requirements for marketing and sales activities articulated in the budget letter. This meant that the managers during the year only had a relatively small proportion of their marketing budget 'free' to spend on unplanned events; the rest was allocated to activities specified in advance, determined by requirements written in the budget letter from HQ and in the budget planning process. The managers were not allowed to exceed the costs planned in the budget, because of the tight focus on keeping within the limit of OPEX. The second problem was related to reporting performance to HQ through their accounting system; the accounting department in Disability Corp. Denmark reported budget performance every month to Disability Tech. Holding HQ. The accounting system in Disability Corp. Denmark and that in Disability Corp. International/Disability Tech. Holding were not identical. Therefore, the accounting system in Denmark and that in HQ were not linked and the numbers needed to be reported manually by one of the Danish accountants. This process was not possible to automate due to some technical shortcomings in the Danish system, which was very old. This implied that HQ would only get aggregated numbers, and therefore, they could not analyze tendencies on a detailed level, in the same way as they did on other subsidiaries that had the same accounting system as HQ. HQ was therefore not able to understand the particular things that went on in the Danish market, and, therefore, their arguments and suggestions were not considered appropriate. The Danish managers perceived the activities that HQ suggested as unnecessary interventions that diverted the managers' time to unproductive activities, and their time was already limited.

This shows how their actions on accounting calculations worked; a larger and larger distance between the performance numbers and the actual unfolding of the market emerged, and HQ acted upon the information they had available in the accounting system, which was detached from the actual sales conditions in the market. Therefore, even though the managers act on the same information as HQ, from a Deleuzian perspective of representation, the difference in how these are signified and which actions ought to be taken lies within the regimes of signs that together form the meaning of the information. In HQ, the assemblage of financial indicators territorializes the meaning they assign to the information, and, thus, the managerial actions perceived necessary. This differed from the understanding the Danish managers have, as they signified the performance numbers by relating the numbers to the markets, including customers and competitors, they act within. One manager expressed it this way:

NJL: Let's talk about reporting. Which reports and which information you use in your work.

SALES MANAGER: Every report I get is based on old customer data and that is reports sent to Germany as well and they are not edited. It is the same reports as we used last year too and because of the municipal merger last year a lot of those customers…

NJL: What do you mean when you say they are not edited?

SALES MANAGER: The information is in fact good enough. The problem is that in the report I get look like there is a lot of decrease here and there. If there isn't any sale; No. that's because the customer does not exist anymore. And that is because the accounting system queries accounts that have had activity within the last two years. That means red, red, red, red, red, red [red numbers in the accounting statements means a negative value, i.e. losses]. And that is not how it actually is. It is not because we are falling behind on reporting, it is because our market in Denmark is so hard to identify. Who are the customers, how do they pay, who are you going to meet and so on. It has actually taken me a whole year to figure that out and as late as yesterday the CFO and I had a meeting where I told him which future reports I need and how they must be built.

(Interview, January 2011)

The manager indicated that the complexity of the Danish system was higher than that of the rest of Europe. In Denmark, her direct customers were public sector branches, but end users are citizens. The payment would come from a central office in the state, and they set the rules about how and when payments are going through. Therefore, to make information useful (for informing aggregately about past sales), it was not reasonable to use the same reporting templates as other countries did, because in other countries end users and customers would be the same individuals. This problem was further complicated because the 'real world' moved, while the reporting template was more static. Therefore, the reports signified problems to HQ that were not actual:

SALES MANAGER: Something [a customer, pseudonym Denmark Physio] that used to have the name [pseudonym Physiotherapy Denmark] is today called [Denmark Physio]. Because the reports we send to Germany and because we are not entirely meeting the sales targets – neither my product line or [Disability Corp. Denmark] as a whole – they are micromanaging down there. They are saying "hey they are not visiting [Physiotherapy Denmark]". No we aren't because we visit [Denmark Physio], which is exactly the same. We are using very much time on different explanations all the time, we are using much time on the explanations because the reports are not transparent.

(Interview, January 2011)

The product manager talked about the interventions from HQ when the monthly profit-loss statement differs from the planned targets. In such situations, the managers were controlled through HQ's significa-tion of the profit/loss statement; a signification they did not believe in themselves. But they would be under pressure to obey the orders from HQ even though they found these were not justifiable based on the Danish managers knowledge of the market. These problems deterrito-rialized the accountability assemblage further because the managers' actions were framed and justified by HQ on the basis of the signifi-cance HQ produced for the accounting information. Therefore, the managers' freedom to act on the specific knowledge about the market was reduced by these interventions from HQ.

Another implication of this is about opportunity. HQ acted as if the budget alone constituted the opportunity space, by acting based on the information only, but the manager expressed that it would be more beneficial to consider opportunity to be present outside the boundaries of the accounting information. This understanding means that opportunity exists in the market, and financial infor-mation is a translation of the transactions that happen in market (which again was the effects of the managerial actions the manag-ers performed). The managers' decision space is therefore influenced tremendously by whether the financial effects signaled progress or recession:

NJL: I thought they let the subsidiaries decide a lot of things themselves?
SALES MANAGER: Yes. In times with progress.
NJL: Ok.
SALES MANAGER: Then they (the subsidiaries) are allowed to make decisions. When there are no progress, corporate decides everything.
SALES MANAGER: The CEO wanted to hire business men. And we want some things, we see some markets, we see something ... We are a very, very special country if you compare with the rest of the world ... They listen to us and what we say but they do not give in.
(Interview, January 2011)

Managers were meant to have a close connection with the market. But when things started to move contradictory to the plan for various reasons; HQ intervened by pressing managers to undertake certain activities without considering the local circumstances that explained the differences between the plan and the actualization of the financial results. The effect of this was that the space of possible managerial actions was reduced more and more, which deterritorialized the managerial possibilities and transformed the accountability of managers into a new, more constrained, expression.

Compromising accountability: utilizing the marketing budget to exploit market movements

The deterritorialization of managerial accountability went further and did not stop there. Another instance that was important for the space of possible managerial actions and the rights to spend money happened in 2011.

The manager responsible for the Disability Corp. High-Tech product line, which in terms of revenue was the largest product line in Disability Corp. Denmark, had been employed in the company for many years. He was a physiotherapist by training, and it was hard for him to become the kind of 'manager' the new budgeting practice pushed him toward becoming.

Late in the summer of 2010, he went on sick leave because of stress. The CFO said that it was probably because of the new budgeting practice that put too much pressure on him, and as a solution to the absent manager, the CEO was appointed as temporary manager for Disability Corp. High-Tech. In the fall of 2010, the CEO found that the sales in Disability Corp. Denmark were becoming a problem and therefore had to do something. He decided to use a large proportion of the marketing budget on a big launch for a new product in the Disability Corp. High-Tech product line. Disability Corp. High-Tech made up approximately 80 percent of the annual sales, and, therefore, the CFO argued that it would be a good place to spend some money, if this meant that they could generate sales growth from the event.

However, Disability Corp. Denmark had strict rules issued by HQ not to exceed their budgeted OPEX. Because of this OPEX rule, the decision of spending marketing money on the product launch generated a new problem. The CEO's spending also needed money from the other managers' marketing budgets in order to keep within the budgeted OPEX level, and therefore, the marketing spending on the activity meant that he used money from the other product managers' marketing budgets. The consequence was that the other managers could not spend money maintaining relations to their customers or start activities they found important for generating further revenue growth in their own product lines.

This also had consequences for the (de)territorialization of the accountability assemblage. The managers were still held responsible for the budget they had planned prior to the financial year, and because of the CEO's two positions in Disability Corp. Denmark (CEO and product manager), one of the managers said that they interpreted the decision as the CEO exploiting his hierarchical power (as CEO) to promote the product line he himself was responsible for (as temporary product manager) (Interview, January 2011). In a later interview, another manager reflected more broadly on the decision and proposed that it could actually be that this event was the best alternative use of the money for Disability Corp. Denmark. However, this manager was responsible for another product line, which organization-wise belonged to a separate legal entity, and therefore, the decision to spend the money did not affect his budget, as it was part of the other entity's financial planning and not Disability Corp. Denmark's financial planning (Interview, September 2011).

This episode is also about the right to spend money and acting on the particular movements in the market. The CEO broke away from the marketing plans. But if the plans were considered to be 'wrong', why not break away from them? From the other managers' perspective, the managers who were affected by his decision, the question they struggled with was whether the CEO acted opportunistically or whether it actually *was* the best decision in the firm's interest. The OPEX number had apparently gained such a privileged place that it was able to deterritorialize the accountability of the marketing budgets and move some of the budgeted money from other managers to the CEOs (acting as a product manager for Disability Corp. High-Tech at the time) spending. If the overall OPEX budget had not been set as a maximum level they must keep within, the CEO could have chosen to spend more than they had planned without compromising how other managers felt that it was to 'be accountable' in this firm.

This matter is also connected with opportunity and whether opportunity lies within or outside the assemblage of calculations. The peculiar aspect of this is that the CEO actually managed to disregard the accounting information, because he found it unrepresentative for how the reality they acted within developed and thought about opportunities outside the boundaries the budget provided.

This incident shows how the OPEX performance indicator deterritorialized the version of accountability that the budget technology assembled. The OPEX indicator created new organizational concerns, which did not preexist before this new assemblage. Put differently, the OPEX indicator had not only accounting representational properties but also organizing and economizing properties, which resulted in deterritorializing and adjudicating effects (Miller & Power, 2013). In Deleuzian language, OPEX occasioned a reconfiguration of the flow of money (a line of flight) that moved accountability into another becoming, and this restricted other managers' possibilities of starting new marketing activities by spending their money. In this way, the OPEX rule, together with the point that the CEO had a credit card that he could use without permission from others, obstructed the ideal of decision freedom within the boundaries of the responsibility center design, by removing the decision opportunities to moving the possibility of spending marketing money from the other managers.

Notes

1 The empirical material in Chapter 5 and this chapter comes from a larger research project, which has been published in the *Scandinavian Journal of Management*. Some portions of the text, such as interview excerpts, have previously been published in "Lennon, N. J. (2019). Responsibility accounting, managerial action and 'a counter-ability': Relating the physical and virtual spaces of decision-making. *Scandinavian Journal of Management, 35* (3), 101062" (with permission from Elsevier).

2 The budget letter for 2011/2012 was not accessible, and, therefore, it is not possible to see how the requirements for the 2011/2012 budget were set. But when asking the CFO (who had quit his job at Disability Corp. in the meantime), he responded

my memory tells me that the growth targets was not specified on departments/product lines, but the expectation was one aggregated increase for the whole subsidiary. How the growth in sales should be divided was a matter for the individual local CEO but exposed to severe discussions with sales managers etc. in [Disability Corp. International], especially when the increase was not perceived as big enough from the group's perspective.

References

Merchant, K. A. (2006). Measuring general managers' performances: Market, accounting and combination-of-measures systems. *Accounting, Auditing & Accountability Journal, 19*(6), 893–917.

Miller, P., & Power, M. (2013). Accounting, organizing, and economizing: Connecting accounting research and organization theory. *The Academy of Management Annals, 7*(1), 557–605.

Epilogue

Absolute deterritorialization of responsibility accounting

This book has concentrated on accounting representativeness, responsibility and accountability and how theoretical concepts from Deleuze's scholarship can mobilize new ways to comprehend the emergent effects of accounting. I have studied and theorized the appropriation of responsibility accounting and how the performance of responsibility accounting can change in relation to the assemblage that constitutes the responsibility center design, when it unfolds in a practical context.

Chapters 5 and 6 described different episodes within our study of how responsibility centers unfold as a performative effect of an assemblage and how this unfolding in practice shapes the managers' decision opportunities. The particular circumstances of market movements, internal accounting principles and cost and revenue concerns show how responsibility accounting is a fragile ideal, especially when implemented in a practical setting. The accountability of managers within the responsibility accounting setup is contested by many different, heterogeneous elements that come together in practice. Thus, the chapters showed that emphasizing a certain responsibility design as an a priori explanation of accountability and decision-making was contested by these various elements. Further, this influenced decision-making in the responsibility center, meaning that the accountability of the managers became fragile and easily compromised by other accounting elements such as credit card spending and transfer prices.

The empirical storyline also shows how the meaning of accounting calculations is not inherently constructed as an effect of the composition of the calculation but by the relations that constitute the assemblage, which the users of accounting calculations act within. Therefore, different significations of the calculations were present between different time-spaces (i.e. different assemblages) when people engaged with the calculations to become informed about the performance of the profit center or informed about their area of responsibility. In Deleuzian and Guattarian terms, the existence of different significations arises from different *regimes of significations* that challenge other meanings and thereby create the possibility of different lines of flight (Deleuze & Guattarí, 2004). These lines of flight are strategic in the sense that they produce lines of possible actions. The empirical episodes illustrate that the regimes of signification are composed of various structural elements, which can be both external to the company and internal to the company, and different managerial concerns such as cost, return on investment and revenue levels. Altogether, these shape the signification of the accounting information, the managerial actions and thus how the decision space of the company emerges in practice.

Managerial emptiness

In the case study, two main managerial concerns are at stake – the concern articulated by headquarters (HQ) and the concern articulated by the Danish management team. HQs' concern is focused on profitability and financial effects in key ratios. This concern is articulated in the transfer pricing practice, operating expenditure (OPEX) rules and budget letter. The concern articulated by the Danish management team is about generating short-term and long-term profit in a market where the conditions are continually changing. These changes lead to decisions that, in some instances, require more free capital than the managers have. Most of their capital is earmarked to certain activities, and they are not in a position where they can relocate funds to other activities. When the two concerns collide, they create a space of managerial, or rational, emptiness – that is, a space without fixed or settled meanings and where rationality is up for grabs (Foucault, 1984; Heede, 1992).

Thus, emptiness, as a conceptual notion, goes in two directions. First, it shows how managers and their managerial beliefs at the very beginning are interiorly empty, but become filled by the assemblage and regimes of signs that the manager acts within and is exposed to. The managers constitute an image of the reality that they perform and act upon, which is constituted based on the assemblage they act through in their daily life. Therefore, their everyday presence in the market through customer visits, their information about competitors' actions and their own accounting information together form this assemblage, which is empty without these elements. Second, in relation to accounting and calculating, emptiness underlines the point that no essence of accounting signs exists within the interior boundaries of calculations. Conflicting significations of the calculations always exist, and these significations co-construct the assemblage in which the managers make decisions about actions to take. This means that how to act responsibly and make appropriate decisions is constituted by both the elements of the assemblage that managers act through and the significations and counter-significations of the accounting numbers – what do they actually express?

Therefore, in some episodes, emptiness emerges in a form where managers do not know what to do; because different regimes of signs constitute the meaning of the sign differently, the notion of emptiness emphasizes that meaning is never given in advance. This means that managers do not know which decisions are most appropriate because the decisions, which are justified as 'good' in one regime (locally in Denmark), can easily be considered 'bad' in the other regime (HQ in Germany). When these two significations collide, which they did in the case studies in Chapters 5 and 6, an emptiness emerges that problematizes and works to deterritorialize the regime's internal consistency; this is what Deleuze and Guattarí call 'lines of active destruction' where the assembled lines of actions become problematized and changed, or perhaps even broke down (Deleuze & Guattarí, 2004, Chapter 12). This concern indicates how regimes of signs are strategic in the way that they co-construct the direction of actions that can be both straightforward or surprising if we relate them to normative principles that constitute the responsibility center design.

Lines of active destruction – absolute deterritorialization

At the end of the case study, the deterritorialization of the managerial practices was taken to the extreme. This started as a consequence of the encounter between the structures of responsibility accounting and the dynamic nature of the practice, where a paradox emerged around HQ's decision rights structures, which were challenged by the way the company calculated the monthly reporting templates and the transfer prices, for example (further explained in Chapter 5). The implication of the findings in the case study is that responsibility accounting only works if this structural element is not taken too seriously. The consequences of HQ's insistence on imposing this structured calculative space meant that, in the spring of 2011, the CFO, who was responsible for the way accountability had materialized in numbers and managerial reports, went on sick leave for two weeks. According to him, the job turned out to be distinctly different from what he had been told prior to taking the position. When he came back, he had decided to quit his job. He explained:

CFO: The most important reason for me to quit is that I should never have started. [short break] The preconditions were not what I expected. My more or less good friend [the CEO] had over-promoted the job. And they did that too in Germany when I visited them to talk about the job. They convinced me there wasn't much financial accounting, more that I should make sure the accounting department in Denmark is doing their tasks and then you must develop the company. With reporting, with general management, with anything, you could say, which is above [day-to-day operations]. As you know it hasn't been possible. And the expectations are that they go more and more in the direction of accounting, accounting, accounting, and reporting to Germany according to the standards they impose on me. It is IFRS standards, but still. All the time here I have thought, OK it is only until we get one or two employees trained to a level where they are self-propelled. But now two years have gone with that and it haven't been successful. Two things can be the reason: it can be the job or it can be the pilot. And I think it is both. In the middle of April it collapsed for me. I went to work a couple of days where I couldn't, I couldn't really remember what I had been doing. Then I took one week to relax, sick leave or what it is called and then, luckily, I had a one week holiday. All in all I had 14 days where I had been away from all of it. And there I realized, OK, it does not fit with me and that job.

(Interview, June 2011)

The marketing manager had also decided to quit in February the same year, because he was weary after working with the CEO. In total, three people, out of nine in the management team, quit their jobs within a period of five months. Eventually another product manager decided to quit too, and, therefore, in mid-2011, four of nine managers had quit their jobs. This could be viewed as the ultimate deterritorialization of the managerial practices in the case company; the resistance against the rigidity of the structure and the regimes of signs that formed the interpretation of managerial performance extended so much so that the managers chose radically different lines of flight by finding other jobs outside the case company. Only one product manager was left in the Copenhagen office, and, therefore, the headquarters office ended up being moved physically to the production and sales department in Jutland, a long away from the Copenhagen office.

This epilogue indicates that the complexity of accountability is difficult to account for – as it is a construction based on the relations of exteriority to other elements in the assemblage – when it comes to expressing what accountability actually is and how it is mobilized in practice. An ideal such as responsibility accounting, which constituted the basis for the managerial accountability structure in the case company, was contested in practice, particularly as the structure had to account for many more elements than it was able to. It is likely that this case study is not unique, as the creation of accountability relations amounts to the act of assembling different elements, which may produce overflows that potentially transform how accounting technologies, such as responsibility accounting, work in practice (see Callon, 1998). Thus, the assemblage always leaves other potentially important elements or concerns out, which is the reason why accountability relationships were framed as processes of territorializing and deterritorializing in this study.

In sum, accounting information constitutes, and engages with, heterogeneous assemblages consisting of relations of exteriority that together change the accounting information itself, as well as the meaning people ascribe to it. These assemblage characteristics were obviously producing problems in terms of the effects the responsibility accounting structures could produce, as well as for the daily performance and decision-making of the managers who were held accountable for their performance through the accounting numbers.

References

Deleuze, G., & Guattarí, F. (2004). *A Thousand Plateaus*. New York, NY: Continuum.

Foucault, M. (1984). Nietzsche, Genealogy, History. In P. Rabinow (Ed.), *The Foucault Reader* (76–100). New York: Pantheon.

Heede, D. (1992). *Det Tomme Menneske*. København: Museum Tusculanums Forlag.

Miller, P. B. (2001). Governing by numbers: Why calculative practices matter. *Social Research, 68*(2), 379–396.

Miller, P. B., & O'Leary, T. (1987). Accounting and the construction of the governable person. *Accounting, Organizations and Society, 12*(3), 235–265.

Index

Note: Page numbers followed by "n" denote endnotes.

Printed in the United States
by Baker & Taylor Publisher Services